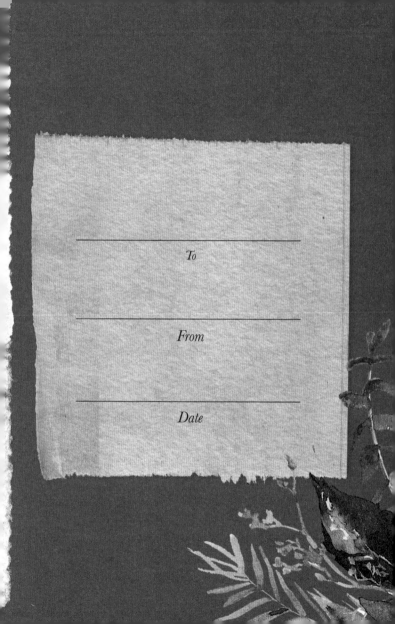

_____

_To_

_____

From

_____

Date

Speaking Power, Love, and Truth
into Your Everyday Life

Words
of *Life*

DaySpring

LIVE YOUR FAITH

Words of Life: Speaking Power, Love, and Truth into Your Everyday Life
Copyright © 2019 by Jennifer Gerelds
First Edition, November 2019

Published by:

DaySpring

P.O. Box 1010
Siloam Springs, AR 72761
dayspring.com

Written by: Jennifer Gerelds
Cover Design: Becca Barnett

Printed in China
Prime: 89901
ISBN: 978-1-68408-629-0

Contents

Introduction

"The Spirit gives life; the flesh counts for nothing. The words I have spoken to you—they are full of the Spirit and life." JOHN 6:63 NIV

I'm sure you know the feeling.... it comes when we step into someone's pain, difficult situation, or defining moment. We want just the right words—but we stand there speechless, totally clueless about what to say. Before we know it, the moment passes, and we're left with the distinct feeling that we missed an opportunity to do the good our Father planned for us to do. If we had been bolder, wiser, or more willing to reach out, perhaps we could have brought the hope or perspective our loved one needed most in that pivotal moment.

We need supernatural help when we have an opportunity to talk about matters of the soul. God's ways are not ours and His thoughts are much higher too. How can we possibly point others to Him and offer valuable encouragement without first consulting Him and His Word?

Words of Life is a resource designed to help us think and speak like Jesus. So in those hard moments, when we don't know what to say, we can speak plainly and purposefully, with divine power, truth, and love. We can know we followed through with just the right words at just the right time to comfort the hearts of those around us. And we can lead people to the Source of peace, joy, and courage, no matter what they may be facing.

Words of Life for the
Lonely

You know how it feels because you've been there yourself. At times in life, our souls ache for connection, for being seen and known in a way that our casual, often hurried interactions can't touch. In fact, feeling alone even when we're surrounded by many people can cause hurt, though we rarely mention it.

Occasionally, desperation gives voice to the hurt and those who feel safest with us divulge their heart's secret: *I am lonely*. How can we encourage them the most? We know our own presence can't solve their deepest need. Fortunately, our Savior understands loneliness because He experienced it Himself, and His Word offers timeless insight into truths that help us remember we are never alone.

"Never will
I leave you;
never will
I forsake you."

Hebrews 13:5 NIV

Life-Giving Words
for the *Lonely*

Turn to me and be gracious to me,
for I am lonely and afflicted. PSALM 25:16 NIV

I'm sorry you feel lonely. I'm here for you and God is even nearer,
wrapping you up in His arms of grace. Remember, Jesus promised
that He is with us to the very end of the age. We are never alone.
What's the best time for us to get together?

◇◇◇◇◇◇◇◇◇◇

Jesus often withdrew to lonely places and prayed. LUKE 5:16 NIV

It's in the lonely places where I have felt the Lord's presence
most intensely and heard His voice most clearly.
I'll ask Him to bless you in those same ways.

◇◇◇◇◇◇◇◇◇◇

[Hagar] gave this name to the LORD who spoke to her: "You are the God who sees
me," for she said, "I have now seen the One who sees me." GENESIS 16:13 NIV

Hagar thought she was alone, but God was there all along,
not only seeing her in her need but ready to answer when she
called out for help. God sees you too, and will rescue
you at the right time when you call out to Him.

◇◇◇◇◇◇◇◇◇◇

Jacob was left alone, and a man wrestled
with him till daybreak. GENESIS 32:24 NIV

We may feel alone wrestling with God in the darkness
like Jacob did, but in the struggle, God blessed Jacob
and changed him forever. God will do the same with you.

*[The woman who had been bleeding for twelve years] came up behind Him
and touched the edge of His cloak, and immediately her bleeding stopped.
"Who touched Me?" Jesus asked. When they all denied it, Peter said, "Master,
the people are crowding and pressing against You." But Jesus said, "Someone
touched Me; I know that power has gone out from Me."* LUKE 8:44-46 NIV

Only those who dare to draw near to God—who dare to have
a personal encounter with Him—get to experience His power
inside them. Loneliness isn't a limitation; it's an invitation
to draw closer to Jesus without the crowds interfering.

∞∞∞∞∞∞∞∞

*God sets the lonely in families,
He leads out the prisoners with singing.* PSALM 68:6 NIV

You aren't alone. Your situation is a family matter!
And God's children—all of us—are ready to stand
with you and see you through this.

∞∞∞∞∞∞∞∞

*The LORD Almighty is with us;
the God of Jacob is our fortress.* PSALM 46:7 NIV

Everywhere you go, you walk hand in hand with the
Lord Almighty who loves you. You will never be alone.

∞∞∞∞∞∞∞∞

*[The Sovereign LORD] gathers the lambs in His arms
and carries them close to His heart.* ISAIAH 40:11 NIV

I love that God sees us as His lambs and cuddles us close to
His heart. Though the world around us might feel cold and
distant, God's love is firm, and His embrace is strong.

Words of Life for the
Brokenhearted

The poor mother had no idea what to do. Her cart was full of groceries, yet unpurchased, and her toddler was wailing at the top of his lungs. A missed naptime for him now meant misery for all the onlookers as, either staring in judgment or cringing in discomfort, they stood in line behind her. After all, who likes to hear babies crying?

For that matter, who likes to hear us cry? Or how do we respond when someone we love is upset about something, whether it's something significant or (from our perspective) seemingly trivial? Sadness doesn't really fit well in our hectic, fast-paced culture. We like to offer quick fixes and hope the heart's cry quiets down quickly so we don't have to feel uncomfortable any longer.

But Jesus had a different way with heartbroken people. We see His real heart in the story of Lazarus. Jesus didn't just send words of comfort from far away; He Himself entered into the grief. Though Jesus knew He would soon raise Lazarus from the dead, Jesus' heart still broke as He felt the weight of His friends' pain. Jesus *wept*!

When we encounter someone who is brokenhearted, let's follow Jesus' example. While it's tempting to offer quick solutions, let's sit with them instead and say with our own tears how much we care for them.

The LORD is near the brokenhearted; He saves those crushed in spirit.

Psalm 34:18

Life-Giving Words
for the *Brokenhearted*

When Joseph came to them in the morning, he saw that they looked distraught.
So he asked Pharaoh's officers who were in custody with him in his master's house,
"Why do you look so sad today?" GENESIS 40:6-7

I've noticed you've been going through a lot lately.
Are you okay? Do you want to talk about it?

∞∞∞∞∞∞∞

The LORD is near the brokenhearted;
He saves those crushed in spirit. PSALM 34:18

It may feel like no one cares or can even help right now,
but I'm here—and God is even closer.

∞∞∞∞∞∞∞

The king said to [Nehemiah], "Why are you sad, when you aren't sick?
This is nothing but sadness of heart."
I was overwhelmed with fear and replied to the king, "May the king live forever!
Why should I not be sad when the city where my ancestors are buried lies
in ruins and its gates have been destroyed by fire?" NEHEMIAH 2:2-3

I can tell you're really upset right now. I'm so sorry. Do you want
to talk about what's hurting the most? If you're willing to trust me,
I'm here to listen. No judgment, I promise. .

∞∞∞∞∞∞∞

"Father, if You are willing, take this cup away from Me—
nevertheless, not My will, but Yours, be done." LUKE 22:42

I am so sorry that you didn't get the _____ you wanted.
Closed doors can feel so hard and abrupt. Trust Jesus with your
hurt and confusion and keep your eyes on Him.
He promises good to those who love Him.

He heals the brokenhearted and bandages their wounds. PSALM 147:3

God doesn't just offer us bandages for our wounds.
His power heals broken bodies and souls from the inside out
because He cares about every part of us!

∞∞∞∞∞∞∞

*The Spirit of the Lord GOD is on Me, because the LORD has anointed Me
to bring good news to the poor. He has sent Me to heal the brokenhearted,
to proclaim liberty to the captives and freedom to the prisoners;
to proclaim the year of the LORD's favor, and the day of our God's vengeance;
to comfort all who mourn, to provide for those who mourn in Zion;
to give them a crown of beauty instead of ashes, festive oil instead of mourning,
and splendid clothes instead of despair. And they will be called righteous trees,
planted by the LORD to glorify Him.* ISAIAH 61:1-3

God has declared His purpose for you: He will heal your heart,
anoint you with His love, and set your soul free
to experience the fullness of His joy!

∞∞∞∞∞∞∞

*Many of the older priests, Levites, and family heads, who had seen
the first temple, wept loudly when they saw the foundation of this temple,
but many others shouted joyfully.* EZRA 3:12

I can only imagine how hard it is to see everyone else seem
so happy while you're walking through such sadness. Just know
I see and remember your hurt and I am here for you.

∞∞∞∞∞∞∞

*Godly grief produces a repentance that leads to salvation without
regret, but worldly grief produces death.* II CORINTHIANS 7:10

Regret makes our failures feel so final. But Jesus
can transform anything. Every time we turn to Him,
He takes our worst mistakes, washes us clean,
and gives us power to start fresh.

15

Words of Life for the
Victorious

In the South, you have to choose a football team. To put it mildly, the sport is big in these parts. Whether or not your team wins can have a surprisingly profound impact on how high you hold your head after a game against your arch rival. Even though your hands never touched the football, you feel the wins and losses because of your allegiance and the identity that stems from it.

As Christians all over the world, we are more than mere spectators or fans watching something dynamic unfold. If we are following Christ, we are actually on the field in this game called Life. Every one of us is a designated offensive and defensive player as we battle the evil in ourselves as we seek to know the Lord and save the lost. But the fight is fierce and it's important that we encourage each other to stay alert, to keep up the good fight, and to celebrate every little win we see along the way. Don't let the sin of comparison keep you from being a team player. Today, ask God to help you recognize the work He is doing in the lives around you and call out each little victory you see. Thank God for every glimpse of His power you see in His people.

Thanks be to God!
He gives us the
victory through
our Lord
Jesus Christ.

I Corinthians 15:57 NIV

Life-Giving Words
for the *Victorious*

The LORD your God is the One who goes with you to fight for you against your enemies to give you victory. DEUTERONOMY 20:4

Remember, you aren't in this alone. God Himself will go before you and literally hand you the victory as you move forward in obedience to Him.

◇◇◇◇◇◇◇◇◇◇◇◇◇

[David] took his life in his hands when he struck down the Philistine [Goliath], and the LORD brought about a great victory for all Israel. You saw it and rejoiced, so why would you sin against innocent blood by killing David for no reason? I SAMUEL 19:5

I saw how you really put yourself out there trusting God like that, and it encouraged my faith. I'm praising God today for what you did.

◇◇◇◇◇◇◇◇◇◇◇◇◇

Let us shout for joy at your victory and lift the banner in the name of our God. May the LORD fulfill all your requests. Now I know that the LORD gives victory to His anointed; He will answer him from His holy heaven with mighty victories from His right hand. PSALM 20:5-6

I am so impressed by the way you are using your gifts and talents to help others. May God make all your efforts prosper as you continue to serve Him!

◇◇◇◇◇◇◇◇◇◇◇◇◇

They did not take the land by their sword—their arm did not bring them victory— but by Your right hand, Your arm, and the light of Your face, because You were favorable toward them. PSALM 44:3

Since God has called you to this situation, He will bring about the victory. Stand strong in Him and watch for His deliverance.

I do not trust in my bow, and my sword does not bring me victory.
But You give us victory over our foes and let those
who hate us be disgraced. PSALM 44:6-7

I know it looks like evil is getting the upper hand, but God has
already won this war. No one who has ever put their hope in Him
has been put to shame—and you won't be the first.

∞∞∞∞∞∞∞

They have greatly oppressed me from my youth,
but they have not gained the victory over me. PSALM 129:2 NIV

Don't let your past keep you from moving toward what God has for
your future. Instead, let God heal your hurts with His love and use
your experience to help others more clearly see His grace.

∞∞∞∞∞∞∞

The LORD takes delight in His people;
He crowns the humble with victory. PSALM 149:4 NIV

You might feel like you're just doing the same thing day after day,
and may wonder if you're making any difference at all
in this big world. But I see God shining in your diligence,
and He will reward your perseverance!

∞∞∞∞∞∞∞

A horse is prepared for the day of battle,
but victory comes from the LORD. PROVERBS 21:31

You've done excellent work planning and preparing and now
we'll watch God work. Together, let's commit these plans
to Him and see what He'll do!

Words of Life for the
Engaged Couple

You may have watched the romance from the very beginning. The happenstance of "I met her at the gym" came to be seen as the work of God bringing two souls together. Watching their love for each other brings joy to everyone around them. Something in our souls knows that marriage is sacred. It is God's design for the human beings He created... He knows what we need.

So what can we say to a giddy couple so full of life and love? Seasoned veterans of marriage may want to venture beyond the typical "Congratulations!" They may even be tempted to warn the lovebirds about the work involved in a healthy marriage or the potential potholes in the road to deepening intimacy. And these concerned onlookers wouldn't be wrong to do so.

But we can both celebrate the event and offer wisdom by speaking blessings over their future union. Blessings and prayers that focus on God's involvement and the importance of Him being at the center of the relationship. Fairytale romance can't stand up to life's harsh realities, but the Holy Spirit's power is greater than any hardship or challenge! Let's encourage any engaged couple we know to build their marriage on the solid foundation of God's love and truth.

As a groom rejoices
over his bride,
so your God will
rejoice over you.

Isaiah 62:5

Life-Giving Words for the *Engaged Couple*

*Let love be without hypocrisy. Detest evil; cling to what is good.
Love one another deeply as brothers and sisters. Outdo one another
in showing honor.* ROMANS 12:9-10

May your love always be wholehearted and grounded
in the Lord—and don't ever stop trying to outdo the other
in acts of service and honor!

∞∞∞∞∞∞∞∞∞

*Give thanks to the LORD, for He is good;
His faithful love endures forever.* I CHRONICLES 16:34

I pray that you will more fully understand God's faithfulness
and love as you embark on this new adventure together!

∞∞∞∞∞∞∞∞∞

*These three remain: faith, hope, and love—
but the greatest of these is love. I* CORINTHIANS 13:13

People will give you lots of advice about marriage, but I can
sum it with a simple sentence: Commit yourselves to loving
each other no matter what the personal cost.

∞∞∞∞∞∞∞∞∞

*Two are better than one because they have a good reward for their efforts.
For if either falls, his companion can lift him up; but pity the one who falls
without another to lift him up.* ECCLESIASTES 4:9-10

As God Himself announced, "It is not good for man [or woman]
to be alone"! I'm so excited that He has blessed you
with each other to journey through life together with Jesus.

Wherever you go, I will go, and wherever you live, I will live;
your people will be my people, and your God will be my God. RUTH 1:16

Marriage is a God-ordained miracle that takes two souls
and unites them as one. This amazing bond gives us a glimpse
into the glory of our union with God.

❦

Be imitators of God, as dearly loved children, and walk in love,
as Christ also loved us and gave Himself for us, a sacrificial
and fragrant offering to God. EPHESIANS 5:1-2

Marriage is a rich journey into trusting God better together. I'm
asking Jesus to walk with both of you each step of the way.

❦

What God has joined together, let no one separate." MATTHEW 19:6

Be on guard against anything steals your time, grabs your attention,
or threatens your devotion to one another. Keep your eyes focused
on God and go to Him together daily in prayer for protection, for
wisdom, for anything and everything on your hearts and minds.

❦

A man who finds a wife finds a good thing
and obtains favor from the LORD. PROVERBS 18:22

May God fill your hearts with His joy as you
daily enjoy each other's love.

❦

Love never ends. I CORINTHIANS 13:8

The time and effort you invest in loving others is an
investment in eternity. Labor to love your spouse well.

Words of Life for the
Uncertain

Career paths. Dating options. Even endless food options in the grocery store! Life, on a daily basis, is full of choices and decisions. How do we know where to go and what to do?

Some of us just like to fly by the seat of our pants and we go in whatever direction feels right in the moment. Others of us like to calculate with more precision, ensuring a sound and well-researched path. Emotions, logic, or some blend of the two seem to lead most of the people on this planet as they search for their best path.

But God's people are different. Though we are all like sheep who can easily wander away from the Shepherd, we don't have to wonder if we're doing the right thing. Unlike the lost sheep, we can choose to follow our faithful and wise Shepherd, Jesus. And if we'll take the time, we'll learn to hear His voice so we can go where He is leading.

So what can we do when people approach us for direction or advice?

While we may be tempted to offer our opinion or immediate gut reaction, we'd do much better to confer with our Creator. God promises that when we acknowledge Him with our wondering about both the big and the small things, He will not just show us the way of wisdom by pointing in the direction He wants us to walk: He'll lead us.

Consider the birds of the sky: They don't sow or reap or gather into barns, yet your heavenly Father feeds them. Aren't you worth more than they?

Matthew 6:26

Life-Giving Words
for the *Uncertain*

Christ is the power of God and the wisdom of God, because God's foolishness is wiser than human wisdom, and God's weakness is stronger than human strength. I CORINTHIANS 1:24-25

Don't worry about what the world will think.
Only God's opinion actually matters.

∘∘∘∘∘∘∘∘∘∘∘∘

"I have filled [the artist Bezalel] with the Spirit of God, with wisdom, with understanding, with knowledge and with all kinds of skills." EXODUS 31:3 NIV

I'm praying that God will fill you with all the creativity and wisdom you need for work and life today!

∘∘∘∘∘∘∘∘∘∘∘∘

The LORD is my shepherd; I have what I need. PSALM 23:1

When we're worried that one wrong move will ruin our lives, we've lost sight of the truth: We will never lack anything we need when we're walking with Jesus.

∘∘∘∘∘∘∘∘∘∘∘∘

Give me wisdom and knowledge, that I may lead this people, for who is able to govern this great people of Yours? II CHRONICLES 1:10 NIV

Parenting is tough and God totally understands.
Ask Him for grace and wisdom. He loves to give us both.

The fear of the LORD is the beginning of wisdom, and the knowledge of the Holy One is understanding. PROVERBS 9:10

When we slow down, sit someplace quiet, and simply remember that God is on the throne, our stress evaporates like the morning dew in the light of the sun.

∞∞∞∞∞∞∞

When pride comes, then comes disgrace, but with humility comes wisdom. PROVERBS 11:2 NIV

God is so faithful! As we humble ourselves and submit to His leading, God always lifts us up.

∞∞∞∞∞∞∞

There is no wisdom, no insight, no plan that can succeed against the LORD. PROVERBS 21:30 NIV

Don't worry. God always wins.

∞∞∞∞∞∞∞

It is God who strengthens us together with you in Christ, and who has anointed us. He has also put His seal on us and given us the Spirit in our hearts as a down payment. II CORINTHIANS 1:21-22

Your salvation doesn't depend on how strong your faith is but on how strong God is. And His power is infinite— He's never letting go of you.

∞∞∞∞∞∞∞

If any of you lacks wisdom, you should ask God, who gives generously to all without finding fault, and it will be given to you. JAMES 1:5 NIV

God won't judge you for not knowing what to do. If you'll ask, He'll gladly give you the light you need to take your next step.

Words of Life for the
Anxious

She couldn't put her finger on the source, really. She began to notice it creeping into every crevice of her life. At work, right before the big meetings; on the drive home, with all the crazy drivers; when she opened the mailbox and saw another bill. The anxiety meter kept inching higher and higher. She could feel it in her stomach... and her soul.

What should she do? What should all of us do? Anxiety seems to plague our nation like never before. Despite the huge uptick in anti-anxiety medicine prescriptions, we still find ourselves frenzied and fretting about so many things. Yet Jesus says, "Fear not!" *But how can we keep from worrying?* we wonder. *Can't He see how huge our problems are?*

Jesus' words are powerful in a way ours aren't. His command comes with supernatural power and the promise of lasting peace. The key? Remembering His presence with us! The God who controls the storm stands with us, ready to steady our hearts even as we start to panic. What hope for us!

And what a breath of fresh air we can bring to those around us when we help them remember our sovereign Savior who quiets the storm with three simple words: *Peace, be still.*

Anxiety in a person's heart weighs it down, but a good word cheers it up.

Proverbs 12:25

Life-Giving Words for the *Anxious*

May the LORD make His face shine on you and be gracious to you;
may the LORD look with favor on you and give you peace. NUMBERS 6:25-26

May God's face and favor shine into every minute,
every second—of your life today.

※※※※※

Remember the days of old; consider the years of past generations.
Ask your father, and he will tell you, your elders,
and they will teach you. DEUTERONOMY 32:7

I love visiting with well-seasoned Christians. Their long time with the
Lord gives them deeper peace because again and again and again,
they've witnessed God's amazing faithfulness.

※※※※※

Gideon built an altar to the LORD there
and called it The LORD Is Peace. JUDGES 6:24

God doesn't just bring us peace. His presence is our peace!
Today I'm asking God to reveal to you His presence with you.

※※※※※

Eli responded, "Go in peace, and may the God of Israel grant
the request you've made of Him." I Samuel 1:17

If you've committed your way to the Lord in prayer,
why pick up your worries again? Leave them at the altar
and watch what miracles God will do.

I will both lie down and sleep in peace,
for You alone, LORD, make me live in safety. PSALM 4:8

Better than any armed soldier, God is always on duty, guarding us
in all our ways. Because He is our Shield and Defender,
we can rest easy. He has us covered.

∞∞∞∞∞∞

Turn away from evil and do what is good; seek peace and pursue it. PSALM 34:14

It's hard to turn away from temptations. I know you will continue
to find strength to seek God and the peace He offers.

∞∞∞∞∞∞

On my bed I remember You; I think of You through
the watches of the night. PSALM 63:6 NIV

I've found that insomnia provides a wonderful opportunity for time
alone with God. At night, focus your thoughts on His throne
and rest in the reality of His presence with you.

∞∞∞∞∞∞

Abundant peace belongs to those who love Your instruction;
nothing makes them stumble. PSALM 119:165

I love how you're holding onto God's promises during this
difficult time. You are an inspiration and a reminder to me
of just how trustworthy God is.

∞∞∞∞∞∞

LORD, You will establish peace for us, for You have also done
all our work for us. ISAIAH 26:12

Our burden is light and we can know peace with God
and peace as we rest in His love because Jesus
did the heavy lifting on Calvary.

Words of Life for the
Depressed

It was all he could do to get out of bed. The moment
the alarm sounded and his eyes opened, the dreaded thoughts
came flooding in like a familiar morning fog. This fog had
darkened the skies of his mind, heart, and hope for months,
leaving him groping for a pathway out. But he still hadn't
found one...

Depression is an inner darkness closing in on us; we can barely
stand up under its weight. Those who haven't experienced
depression find it almost impossible to understand the vise-like
grip it holds on its sufferers. But many of us know firsthand the
terrors that true depression brings. Every day it affects more and
more people, Christians included. It is a weapon our enemy uses
to snuff out the hope and joy God has for His people.

How can we speak words of real encouragement—words of
life—to someone struggling with depression? We are warned
in the book of Job not to judge, criticize, or patronize others
in their pain. Instead, we are simply to be present. We offer
the encouragement of our diligent and persistent friendship.
We listen to the cries of their heart and wait with them in their
darkness for God's light to break through. Ask the Lord for
His Words, His heart, to share in His time, and then wait for
the window of opportunity He will provide. The truth, spoken
gently in love, sets us all free. As God's Word says, "No weapon
forged against us will prevail."

I waited patiently for the LORD,
and He turned to me and heard
my cry for help. He brought me
up from a desolate pit, out of
the muddy clay, and set my feet
on a rock, making my steps secure.
He put a new song in my mouth,
a hymn of praise to our God.
Many will see and fear,
and they will trust in the LORD.

Psalm 40:1-3

Life-Giving Words for the *Depressed*

"No weapon formed against you will succeed, and you will refute any accusation raised against you in court. This is the heritage of the LORD's servants, and their vindication is from Me." This is the LORD's declaration. ISAIAH 54:17

I'm sorry you feel overwhelmed right now. It makes sense with Satan coming so hard against you, but he is not stronger than God who is for you and in you. The light will come!

∞∞∞∞∞∞∞∞∞∞

[The once blind man] replied, "The man they call Jesus made some mud and put it on my eyes. He told me to go to Siloam and wash. So I went and washed, and then I could see." JOHN 9:11 NIV

Sometimes Jesus just gave the command for healing, and other times He used unique methods as He worked His miracle. Jesus uses biblical counseling and medication as a possible means to health and freedom.

∞∞∞∞∞∞∞∞∞∞

The weapons of our warfare are not of the flesh, but are powerful through God for the demolition of strongholds. We demolish arguments and every proud thing that is raised up against the knowledge of God, and we take every thought captive to obey Christ. II CORINTHIANS 10:4-5

The fight in our minds is always the fiercest because the lies we believe sound so convincing to us. But God is right and good. Believe Him and let the truth of His love shield you from every fiery dart the enemy throws your way.

"For I know the plans I have for you"—this is the LORD's declaration—"plans for your well-being, not for disaster, to give you a future and a hope. You will call to Me and come and pray to Me, and I will listen to you. You will seek Me and find Me when you search for Me with all your heart. I will be found by you"—this is the LORD's declaration—"and I will restore your fortunes." JEREMIAH 29:11-14

The doors of this prison won't stay locked forever.
Your freedom will come. Remember, God has promised
He has great plans for you. Just keep clinging to
Jesus and believing His promises. His love will not fail you.

∞∞∞∞∞∞∞

The angel of the LORD returned for a second time and touched [Elijah]. [The angel] said, "Get up and eat, or the journey will be too much for you." I KINGS 19:7

Elijah, one of God's strongest prophets of all time, suffered from depression. But God saw and responded. He sent angels to strengthen Elijah with food and company. You need to eat and get up too—don't isolate yourself. God still has work for you to do.

∞∞∞∞∞∞∞

The father of the boy cried out, "I do believe; help my unbelief!" MARK 9:24

We don't need to try to hide our weakness from God.
He already knows it! We can make this father's prayer our own:
Help my unbelief, Lord God!

∞∞∞∞∞∞∞

As high as the heavens are above the earth, so great is [God's] faithful love toward those who fear Him. As far as the east is from the west, so far has He removed our transgressions from us. PSALM 103:11-12

God's love is a like a grand eraser. He wipes away our past,
present, and future sins and clothes us with
Christ's robe of righteousness.

Words of Life for Those
Who Are Waiting

Wait *is definitely a four-letter word for many of us.*
It seems to be aligned with inefficiency and frustration, ready
to combust into either anger or fear. Few things feel more
uncomfortable or unproductive than the span of time that
exists between where we are and what we desire, whether it's
as small as waiting for a ride in Disney World or as significant
as waiting for the right person to marry.

Every time we wait, we find ourselves in a wilderness of sorts.
We don't know what's going to happen and when, or if life will
turn the way we want it to go. This lack of control fuels a sense
of vulnerability and impatience. We want—and even demand
of God—any kind of motion to assure our souls we won't be
staying in the land of waiting for long.

But God has a history of leading His people into the
wilderness: Think Abraham, Joseph, Moses, David, and *Jesus*.
It's in the waiting, and even wandering, where our hearts get
tested and our faith is refined like gold in a furnace. When we
turn to God in our wilderness, we will find trust growing in
our hearts. In the waiting, our faith grows as we discover that
God is present with us. His presence helps us be more patient
in the process, and we learn to live at peace with Him in faith's
refining fires.

I say, "The LORD is my
portion, therefore I will
put my hope in Him."
The LORD is good to those
who wait for Him,
to the person who seeks Him.
It is good to wait quietly
for salvation from the LORD.

Lamentations 3:24-26

Life-Giving Words for Those *Who are Waiting*

In the morning, LORD, You hear my voice; in the morning I plead my case to You and watch expectantly. PSALM 5:3

When we wake up in the morning, the first item on our daily to-do is to hand over to God all the worries for the day and then wait at His feet until we hear from Him.

<hr>

I am certain that I will see the LORD's goodness in the land of the living. Wait for the LORD; be strong, and let your heart be courageous. Wait for the LORD. PSALM 27:13-14

You can be certain of this: God has good planned for you today, tomorrow, and forever. Just wait and see!

<hr>

We wait for the LORD; He is our help and shield. For our hearts rejoice in Him because we trust in His holy name. PSALM 33:20-21

You not only have a powerful Helper, but He is also shielding you from harm as you wait on Him. He will deliver you at just the right time!

<hr>

Be still before the LORD and wait patiently for Him; do not fret when people succeed in their ways, when they carry out their wicked schemes. Refrain from anger and turn from wrath; do not fret—it leads only to evil. PSALM 37:7-8 NIV

It's so frustrating to see people who hate our God seem to have easy, prosperous, carefree lives. But that's not your worry or mine. We know God promises amazingly good gifts to His children. And sometimes we find a few of those gifts as we wait in a wilderness.

Abundant peace belongs to those who love Your instruction;
nothing makes them stumble. LORD, *I hope for Your salvation*
and carry out Your commands. PSALM 119:165-166

When we're flat on our face before the Father, we can't fall! May God make us hungry for His Word, for prayer time with Him, and for the peace that comes when we humbly obey what we hear Him say to us.

∞∞∞∞∞∞∞∞

I wait for the LORD; *I wait and put my hope in His word.*
I wait for the LORD *more than watchmen for the morning—*
more than watchmen for the morning. PSALM 130:5-6

As certain as the sun rises, God will come to the rescue.
Keep your eyes to the east!

∞∞∞∞∞∞∞∞

Don't say, "I will avenge this evil!" Wait on the LORD,
and He will rescue you. PROVERBS 20:22

There's no need to retaliate or take matters into your own hands.
God always rescues His children—and He will also
deal with those who offended you.

∞∞∞∞∞∞∞∞

The LORD *is waiting to show you mercy, and is rising up*
to show you compassion, for the LORD *is a just God. All who wait*
patiently for Him are happy. ISAIAH 30:18

As your emotions say, "Run!" God's Spirit says, "Wait and feel
the full weight of My favor and love." God is "rising up to
show you compassion" and be with you as you wait.

Words of Life for the
Afraid

The very second that Adam and Eve heard God's footsteps after they had disobeyed Him, they hid. For the first time in their once-perfect lives, they were afraid of God's response to their disobedience, to their sin. Tragically, they feared the response of the One who had loved them most. But sin had caused an unbridgeable division, and all of creation around them experienced that fallout with them.

Adam and Eve quickly discovered that the One whose reaction they feared was more faithful than they ever imagined. Despite their sin, God covered their nakedness—and God extends that same forgiveness and covering to all of His kids.

There's much to fear in this fallen world populated by sinners and invaded by Satan and evil, and God is well aware. More than 300 times in the Old and New Testaments, God tells us, "Do not fear." In addition to issuing that command, He promises His protection and closeness.

If we have put our faith in Christ, we never have to be afraid of our heavenly Father when we stumble and sin. We never have to be afraid of life's circumstances either. Our Father always welcomes us into His presence. Because of His promise to surround, protect, and supply us with all that we need, we can boldly face anything that threatens to undo us. Greater is He who is in us than he who is threatening us in the world!

He who dwells in the
shelter of the Most High
will rest in the shadow
of the Almighty.
I will say of the LORD,
"He is my refuge and
my fortress, my God,
in whom I trust.

Psalm 91:1-2 NIV

Life-Giving Words
for the *Afraid*

Do not fear, for I am with you; do not be afraid, for I am your God.
I will strengthen you; I will help you; I will hold on to you with
My righteous right hand. ISAIAH 41:10

Remember how you felt as a kid when you held Dad or Mom's hand?
That grip gave you the confidence to go where you needed to go. You
might not feel it as concretely when you hold God's hand, but know
that He has you in His faithful grip. And He's not letting go.

<><><><><><><><>

When I am afraid, I will trust in You. PSALM 56:3

Childlike faith means that when we're afraid, we climb into the
warmth and safety of God's strong and loving arms.

<><><><><><><><>

Don't worry about anything, but in everything, through prayer and petition
with thanksgiving, present your requests to God. And the peace of God,
which surpasses all understanding, will guard your hearts
and minds in Christ Jesus. PHILIPPIANS 4:6-7

Lord, thank You for this opportunity to trust You. Though my
knees are shaking, my heart is resting as I choose
to believe in Your sovereign care.

<><><><><><><><>

"Peace I leave with you. My peace I give to you. I do not give to you as
the world gives. Don't let your heart be troubled or fearful." JOHN 14:27

One reason Jesus' peace is different from the world's is,
His peace springs from His Spirit within us. With the Holy Spirit
residing in our hearts, we can know His peace anytime
and anywhere, whatever life's circumstances.

God has not given us a spirit of fear, but one of power, love, and sound judgment. II TIMOTHY 1:7

Cast off your fears by filling your mind with Truth. God's Word teaches that Jesus provides the power, love, and wisdom we need to face the future with confidence.

∞∞∞∞∞∞∞

There is no fear in love; instead, perfect love drives out fear, because fear involves punishment. So the one who fears is not complete in love. I JOHN 4:18

God isn't out to punish you. His wrath toward sin was satisfied by the cross. We live completely loved by God.

∞∞∞∞∞∞∞

This is what the LORD says—the One who created you, Jacob, and the One who formed you, Israel—"Do not fear, for I have redeemed you; I have called you by your name; you are Mine." ISAIAH 43:1

You are not lost or left behind. You, dear child of God, will never be left as an orphan. You are a member of God's forever family.

∞∞∞∞∞∞∞

Haven't I commanded you: be strong and courageous? Do not be afraid or discouraged, for the LORD your God is with you wherever you go. JOSHUA 1:9

Take courage! God goes before you, and He is beside you, within you, and behind you! God's got you covered!

The fear of mankind is a snare, but the one who trusts in the LORD is protected. PROVERBS 29:25

Don't worry about what people are saying. Keep focused on Jesus. Rest in the truth that He will keep you safe.

Words of Life for the
Pessimist

Even as you're driving to work, you already sense the growing dread. It's not the work that bothers you; it's your coworker whose sour attitude about almost everything seems to sap all your energy. You pass by his desk throughout the day, and you're determined to keep conversations with him short, but his negativity still gnaws at you until your own smile starts to fade.

What are we to do with the pessimists in our lives? Avoid them at all costs? Commiserate with their misery just to keep the peace? Offer a more positive perspective?

While we don't have the power to change people's minds, God's Word does! Even when we can't quote Scripture directly, we can breathe life and joy into our environment by knowing, believing, and speaking God's perspective in response to the negativity we encounter.

Speaking truth in love can dispel the faulty thinking and even influence those around you to think differently. Don't avoid that annoying person. Instead, elevate the conversation with divine inspiration and pray for God's Spirit to help the pessimists in your world to get the better, bigger picture!

A cheerful heart
is good medicine,
but a crushed spirit
dries up the bones.

Proverbs 17:22 NIV

Life-Giving Words
for the *Pessimist*

"My thoughts are not your thoughts, neither are your ways My ways,"
declares the LORD. ISAIAH 55:8 NIV

I know this might not look like a good situation, but remember
that God's perspective is so different from ours.
His ways are higher, so let's just see what He has in store.

∞∞∞∞∞∞∞∞

Whatever you do, do it from the heart, as something done for the Lord and not for
people, knowing that you will receive the reward of an inheritance from the Lord.
You serve the Lord Christ. COLOSSIANS 3:23-24

Sure, other people don't always notice our efforts. But God sees
it all—and He's the One we're serving! He is a faithful rewarder.

∞∞∞∞∞∞∞∞

The Lord does not delay His promise, as some understand delay, but is patient
with you, not wanting any to perish but all to come to repentance. II PETER 3:9

Trust God's timing. It's always perfect.

∞∞∞∞∞∞∞∞

Honor everyone. Love the brothers and sisters. Fear God.
Honor the emperor. I PETER 2:17

The boss's delivery style is not my favorite either, but God
put him in authority over us. I know God is with us
and I'm trusting Him to teach us through this experience.

Consider it a great joy, my brothers and sisters, whenever you experience various trials, because you know that the testing of your faith produces endurance. JAMES 1:2-3

I'm so sorry you're having a rough day. I'm asking God right now to help you feel His presence and comfort.

<hr>

I urge that petitions, prayers, intercessions, and thanksgivings be made for everyone, for kings and all those who are in authority, so that we may lead a tranquil and quiet life in all godliness and dignity. I TIMOTHY 2:1-2

We might not always agree with our boss, but we can pray that God will bless our work efforts and remind us to pray for those in charge.

<hr>

There is no Jew or Greek, slave or free, male and female; since you are all one in Christ Jesus. GALATIANS 3:28

We can avoid the comparison trap because Jesus doesn't compare. Actually, Jesus levels the field, declaring us all to be equally in need of His grace and equally loved by the Father.

<hr>

In the morning sow your seed, and at evening do not let your hand rest, because you don't know which will succeed, whether one or the other, or if both of them will be equally good. ECCLESIASTES 11:6

Don't be discouraged! God's plan is still unfolding.

<hr>

Let us not love in word or speech, but in action and in truth. I JOHN 3:18

Would you like to join me in taking them a meal? I know they've caused us some problems, but this is a great opportunity to show them God's love.

Words of Life for Those
Expecting a Child or Hoping for One

The second she saw the blue line appear, she started to shake with excitement. *I'm going to be a mom,* she whispered to herself. First step, tell her husband. Next, her parents. Then, the world. *Will everyone be happy for me? Will they help me find my way in the new terrain of parenting?* The wonder of all that was ahead left her mind swimming with thoughts and her heart overwhelmed with emotion.

It is exciting when people announce they're pregnant. With a new life comes so much potential, so much promise, so much learning. It's also the perfect opportunity to speak blessing over the new little person and to inspire the parents-to-be with God's promises to guide them on this exciting new adventure.

But not every pregnancy or attempt to get pregnant has a happy ending. Despite trying every possible option, some couples can't conceive. Miscarriage or month after month of devastating disappointment shatters dreams and wounds hearts deeply. These are the moments when God-given words can awaken some hope as they wait for their miracle.

Keep yourselves
in the love of God,
waiting expectantly
for the mercy of our
Lord Jesus Christ
for eternal life.

Jude 1:21

Life-Giving Words for Those *Expecting a Child or Hoping for One*

It was you who created my inward parts; You knit me together in my mother's womb. I will praise You because I have been remarkably and wondrously made. Your works are wondrous, and I know this very well. PSALM 139:13-14

God is knitting together a divine miracle, someone He had planned before the beginning of time. What a blessing!

∞∞∞∞∞∞∞

My bones were not hidden from You when I was made in secret, when I was formed in the depths of the earth. Your eyes saw me when I was formless; all my days were written in Your book and planned before a single one of them began. PSALM 139:15-16

God is not surprised by this diagnosis. His ways aren't our ways. They are puzzling and sometimes painful for us, but they are higher and better because He is good. Trust Him to carry you as you carry this precious life inside you.

∞∞∞∞∞∞∞

Take delight in the LORD, and He will give you your heart's desires. Commit your way to the LORD; trust in Him, and He will act. PSALM 37:4-5

God knows you want a baby and He didn't give you that desire to torment you. Pour out your heart to Him. He always hears and answers our prayers according to His goodness, and often in a most surprising way.

After some time, Hannah conceived and gave birth to a son. She named him
Samuel, because she said, "I requested him from the LORD." I SAMUEL 1:20

Rest in God's timing. He doesn't usually answer our prayers
as quickly as we want, but we can experience His peace when
we wait on Him and choose to trust Him.

∞∞∞∞∞∞∞

"Look, I am the LORD, the God over every creature.
Is anything too difficult for Me?" JEREMIAH 32:27

Doctors don't determine our destiny; God does. And nothing
is too hard for Him! Keep your eyes on our Father and
trust Him to take care of you and your little one.
The Creator of the universe is working in you to design
His beautiful masterpiece in His perfect timing.

∞∞∞∞∞∞∞

God blessed them, and God said to them, "Be fruitful, multiply, fill the earth,
and subdue it. Rule the fish of the sea, the birds of the sky,
and every creature that crawls on the earth." GENESIS 1:28

I'm praising God for blessing your family with a new life,
a new little person created in the image of God, and a new
opportunity to experience and learn more about God's love.

∞∞∞∞∞∞∞

Like arrows in the hand of a warrior are the sons born in one's youth.
Happy is the man who has filled his quiver with them. PSALM 127:4-5

God has blessed your family again! I'm praying for
continued guidance and protection as He grows
each one of your children in Him.

Words of Life for Those
Facing Divorce

She never saw it coming... She couldn't have imagined this kind of tearing in her soul. She had never dreamed this would happen to her. *Divorce.*

The very sound of the word seems to ring with condemnation. And it brings to mind nothing good: Failure. Soul separation. Profound pain. Self-doubt rising from deep within. A host of fears for the future. Fears for her family. For survival.

Christians aren't immune to divorce. Even we who love Jesus can find ourselves dealing with treachery, betrayal, abandonment, and infidelity by a partner whose heart left the Lord long ago. Worse yet, these Christians who have gone through a divorce feel they wear a scarlet letter, a symbol of shame obvious in every Christian circle. After a while, they may even choose to avoid believers altogether just to ease the burden of shame.

But there's a better way. Instead of shaming or shunning fellow Christians who are in crisis, we can circle around them with love, not judgment; with acceptance, not rejection; with prayers to bind the enemy's attacks; with the blessing of believing truth for them when they're struggling to find faith on their own. As we live out Christ's love and hope, these hurting people can stand taller and stronger as time goes by. Their stories aren't over yet. Marriages can be saved; lives, healed; and new paths, formed when we take our hurting friends to the feet of Jesus.

Be satisfied with
what you have,
for He Himself
has said, I will
never leave you
or abandon you.

Hebrews 13:5

Life-Giving Words for Those *Facing Divorce*

Be strong, and let your heart be courageous, all you who put your hope in the LORD. PSALM 31:24

I know this is an incredibly difficult time. I'm asking the Lord to give you supernatural peace and strength. Know I'm here for you 24/7.

Let me hear joy and gladness; let the bones you have crushed rejoice. Turn your face away from my sins and blot out all my guilt. PSALM 51:8-9

I can only imagine how crushed you feel right now, but life won't always be like this. I'm believing for you that a day is coming when the Lord will lift your head, and you will feel joy again.

I call to You from the ends of the earth when my heart is without strength. Lead me to a Rock that is high above me, for You have been a Refuge for me, a strong Tower in the face of the enemy. PSALM 61:2-3

I am so sorry for the incredible pain you are experiencing. God promises to be a refuge for all who flee to Him. So I want to pray and ask God to enable you to feel His warm love and sheltering presence surrounding you.

Didn't God make [you and the wife of your youth] one and give them a portion of spirit? What is the one seeking? Godly offspring. So watch yourselves carefully, so that no one acts treacherously against the wife of his youth. MALACHI 2:15

God's Spirit is in you, and He will give you the strength and wisdom you need to fight for your family.

From the beginning of creation God made them male and female.
For this reason a man will leave his father and mother and the two
will become one flesh. So they are no longer two, but one flesh. Therefore what
God has joined together, let no one separate." MARK 10:6-9

Your spouse isn't the greatest enemy you face right now; Satan is.
So let's stand together against his schemes to destroy your marriage.

∞∞∞∞∞∞∞∞∞∞

Jesus replied to [the disciples], "Have faith in God. Truly I tell you,
if anyone says to this mountain, 'Be lifted up and thrown into the sea,'
and does not doubt in his heart, but believes that what he says will happen,
it will be done for him." MARK 11:22-23

Don't give up hope. God is doing a work that we can't see.
Let's pray together that God will turn both your spouse's heart
and yours fully to Him and restore what has been lost.

∞∞∞∞∞∞∞∞∞∞

Give careful thought to do what is honorable in everyone's eyes. If possible, as far
as it depends on you, live at peace with everyone. ROMANS 12:17-18

I can't imagine how difficult this must be for you. So I'm asking
God to give you strength to say life-giving words to your ex.
God will be glorified as your children see His grace
in the way you talk to him/her.

∞∞∞∞∞∞∞∞∞∞

Do not be conquered by evil, but conquer evil with good. ROMANS 12:21

It is so tempting to want to retaliate when people hurt us,
but doing so can make the situation worse. So let's seek
help from the Father. He is able to empower you with
His grace and love to take the high road.

55

Words of Life for
Parents Who Adopt

Whoever said that adopting is easier than enduring a pregnancy clearly has never adopted. Mountains of paperwork, seemingly endless loopholes, and outrageously high bills are some of the labor pains of adoption. Far worse is the agonizing wait once you've seen the one you know in your heart belongs with you!

Even those who haven't experienced adoption firsthand can witness the joyous work of God as He places the lonely in families. Is there any clearer picture of our Father's love than the love that compelled Jesus to leave heaven in order to take on the death sentence for our sins? Jesus' sacrificial love and resurrection victory over sin and death enable us to be in relationship with our holy God as *adopted* members of His forever family.

When we walk alongside those who are adopting, we have the wonderful opportunity to not only pray for the process, but also witness the wonder of God's saving mercy and grace. Proclaim His greatness and faithfulness as you watch and marvel together at the miracle of adoption.

"Whoever welcomes
one child like this
in My name
welcomes Me"

Matthew 18:5

Life-Giving Words for *Parents Who Adopt*

To all who did receive [Jesus], He gave them the right to be children of God, to those who believe in His name, who were born, not of natural descent, or of the will of the flesh, or of the will of man, but of God. JOHN 1:12-13

Adoption was on God's heart from the very beginning of time! So you are walking in our Father's footsteps!

∞∞∞∞∞∞∞∞

"Whatever you ask in My name, I will do it so that the Father may be glorified in the Son." JOHN 14:13

I will pray and wait with you for our Father to choose the child He wants to join your family.

∞∞∞∞∞∞∞∞

All those led by God's Spirit are God's sons. For you did not receive a spirit of slavery to fall back into fear. Instead, you received the Spirit of adoption, by whom we cry out, "Abba, Father!" ROMANS 8:14-15

Let God's perfect love drive out any fear you have. Know that He loves you and the child you are adopting/have adopted. He will guide you, provide for you, and bless you as you adopt, just as He adopted you.

∞∞∞∞∞∞∞∞

The Spirit Himself testifies together with our spirit that we are God's children, and if children, also heirs—heirs of God and coheirs with Christ—if indeed we suffer with Him so that we may also be glorified with Him. ROMANS 8:16-17

God uses suffering to shape us more into Christ's image. As your family struggles to bond and heal, I'm asking Him to help your hearts find an anchor in His divine plan and His promise to bless you.

58

*I speak as to my children; as a proper response,
open your heart to us.* II Corinthians 6:13

I'm asking the Father to open your child's heart
to you as well as to the love of Jesus.

◇◇◇◇◇◇◇◇◇◇

*[God] predestined us to be adopted as sons through Jesus Christ for Himself,
according to the good pleasure of His will, to the praise of His glorious grace that
He lavished on us in the Beloved One.* Ephesians 1:5-6

Adoption brings God great pleasure. As He walks alongside you,
He'll gladly help you as you learn the ropes and rely on Him.

◇◇◇◇◇◇◇◇◇◇

*Pure and undefiled religion before God the Father is this: to look after orphans and
widows in their distress and to keep oneself unstained from the world.* James 1:27

Even when the going gets tough, remember that God's
got your back. He celebrates and supports those
who share His heart for the lost and lonely.

◇◇◇◇◇◇◇◇◇◇

*God sets the lonely in families, He leads out the prisoners
with singing.* Psalm 68:6 NIV

I'm rejoicing with you. Out of all the families in the world,
God chose you to receive the blessing of this beautiful child.

◇◇◇◇◇◇◇◇◇◇

*Because you are His sons, God sent the Spirit of His Son into our
hearts, the Spirit who calls out, "Abba, Father."* Galatians 4:6 NIV

May you learn to know and trust your Abba Father as this
child God chose for you learns to know and
trust you as his earthly mom and dad.

Words of Life
When We Lose

Breathlessly, she waited for the results. It was her third try to qualify for her bucket list race: the Boston Marathon. Moments later, she knew as did the friends and family members cheering her on. Despite all her months of long, hard training, she still couldn't make the cut. Several runners finished faster, and her best efforts failed. She wasn't sure which was worse: the immediate disappointment or the shame that always came with losing.

But God's view of success is so vastly different from ours. To Him, the only failure is us losing focus on Him. What looks like loss to us is God's formula for true victory. Character forged through failure yields a perseverance that pleases our Savior. When we surrender our dwindling hopes and decimated dreams to His sovereignty, we see beauty rising from the ashes.

But when we're in the throes of defeat, victory is hard to see. That's why God brings us alongside our brothers and sisters who are in the trenches. We can speak to the mystery of God's ways and the goodness of His plans, and we can push our friends from their place of defeat to the feet of our Savior who will ease the hurt and help them to grow from it.

The LORD will
hold your hand,
and if you stumble,
you still won't fall.

Psalm 37:24 CEV

Life-Giving Words for *When We Lose*

He brought me up from a desolate pit, out of the muddy clay, and set my feet on a rock, making my steps secure. He put a new song in my mouth, a hymn of praise to our God. Many will see and fear, and they will trust in the LORD. PSALM 40:2-3

If this setback hadn't happened, people wouldn't get to witness the miraculous redemption God will work through you. Just watch and see!

<small>◇◇◇◇◇◇◇◇◇◇◇◇</small>

You planned evil against me; God planned it for good to bring about the present result—the survival of many people. GENESIS 50:20

God not only has the power to redeem this situation, but He will also use it to bless many others around you.

<small>◇◇◇◇◇◇◇◇◇◇◇◇</small>

Humble yourselves, therefore, under God's mighty hand, that He may lift you up in due time. I PETER 5:6 NIV

I am so proud of you for putting yourself out there and doing your best. Even though you didn't get the results you wanted, your dedication and resilience are truly incredible.

<small>◇◇◇◇◇◇◇◇◇◇◇◇</small>

When God restores the fortunes of His people, let Jacob rejoice, let Israel be glad. PSALM 53:6

If you don't experience the pain of failure, you won't ever know how wonderful God's restoration and redemption really are.

"So I will restore to you the years that the swarming locust has eaten, The crawling locust, The consuming locust, And the chewing locust, My great army which I sent among you. You shall eat in plenty and be satisfied, And praise the name of the LORD your God, Who has dealt wondrously with you; And My people shall never be put to shame." JOEL 2:25-26 NKJV

We may not always win, but if we trust in the Lord, we will never be put to shame. In His time, God turns our trials into triumphs.

∞∞∞∞∞∞∞∞

[The LORD] said to me, "Prophesy concerning these bones and say to them: Dry bones, hear the word of the LORD! This is what the Lord GOD says to these bones: I will cause breath to enter you, and you will live." EZEKIEL 37:4-5

You might think this situation is completely hopeless, but God is in the miracle business. If He can breathe life into dry bones, He can bring beauty out of these ashes.

∞∞∞∞∞∞∞∞

Though a righteous person falls seven times, he will get up, but the wicked will stumble into ruin. PROVERBS 24:16

It's not that we don't fall. All of us do. It's just that Jesus, who holds our hand, keeps the fall from being permanent.

∞∞∞∞∞∞∞∞

"I know your works. Look, I have placed before you an open door that no one can close because you have but little power; yet you have kept My word and have not denied My name." REVELATION 3:8

Don't let this obstacle get you down.
God will open the right door for you at the right time.
Choose to trust Him and wait for Him.

Words of Life for the
Dying

The only thing worse than his diagnosis was having to tell his friends and family. He could already hear the conversation: "Surely there's something they can do. Some trial or special homeopathic remedy they don't know about." Yet he knew that apart from a miracle, he would meet his Maker far sooner than he had ever imagined.

It's interesting that we all know we'll die one day, but we don't like to acknowledge its reality in our day-to-day lives. And when we witness someone nearing death, we don't know what to say.

As believers though, the nearness of death actually opens a door for great discussion. What has God promised those who put their faith in Him? What blessings are ahead? And how can people left behind continue the ministry their loved ones will leave behind?

By the power of the cross, death is not the end of the story. It's the doorway to a heavenly paradise that's promised to and awaits every believer. Let's walk with our family and friends through the shadows of death, knowing our Savior is leading the way to life eternal.

Even when
I go through the
darkest valley,
I fear no danger,
for You are with me.

Psalm 23:4

Life-Giving Words for the *Dying*

The one who has the Son has life. The one who does not have the Son of God does not have life. I have written these things to you who believe in the name of the Son of God so that you may know that you have eternal life. I JOHN 5:12-13

With Jesus as our Savior, we face even death with confidence. To live is Christ, but to die is gain!

※※※※※※※

Christ, having been offered once to bear the sins of many, will appear a second time, not to bear sin, but to bring salvation to those who are waiting for Him. HEBREWS 9:28

We either go to be with Jesus in heaven or we join Him in the clouds when He returns. The future is a win-win for all God's people.

※※※※※※※

[One of the criminals crucified alongside Jesus] said, "Jesus, remember me when You come into Your kingdom." And He said to him, "Truly I tell you, today you will be with Me in paradise." LUKE 23:42-43

Whether we've known Jesus as our Savior and Lord all our life or only for five minutes, He welcomes us into paradise.

※※※※※※※

"Don't let your heart be troubled. Believe in God; believe also in Me. In My Father's house are many rooms; if not, I would have told you. I am going away to prepare a place for you. If I go away and prepare a place for you, I will come again and take you to Myself, so that where I am you may be also." JOHN 14:1-3

It's no wonder Jesus chose carpentry as an earthly trade. It's His divine occupation too! He's building an incredible place for us.

Everyone who calls on the name of the Lord will be saved. ROMANS 10:13

God made salvation so simple. We acknowledge the blood of Jesus
as our means of forgiveness and with this saving grace,
we receive eternity with Him as a free gift.

∞∞∞∞∞∞∞∞∞∞

Don't throw away your confidence, which has a great reward.
For you need endurance, so that after you have done God's will,
you may receive what was promised. HEBREWS 10:35-36

Cling to the God who loves you dearly. Know that
He has seen all you've done in His name, and He will
reward you when you reach heaven.

∞∞∞∞∞∞∞∞∞∞

Let us hold on to the confession of our hope without wavering,
since He who promised is faithful. HEBREWS 10:23

Have you ever tried to count all the promises our God has kept?
More important than the actual number is the fact that
He never fails! He will see you through this valley too.

∞∞∞∞∞∞∞∞∞∞

I am persuaded that neither death nor life, nor angels nor rulers,
nor things present nor things to come, nor powers, nor height nor depth,
nor any other created thing will be able to separate us from the love of God
that is in Christ Jesus our Lord. ROMANS 8:38-39

Nothing you have done or will do can change God's love for you.
You are permanently and forever His child, whom He loves
dearly and with whom He looks forward to sharing eternity.

Words of Life for
Nervous Friends

It's just a few hours away until the show starts, but the leading actress can't calm her nerves. *What if I mess up? What if I can't remember my lines? What if I blow the whole thing?* Worries race through her mind, wreaking havoc on her stomach. She can't seem to slow down the mounting tension.

Even the most confident people experience nervousness. Sometimes we have to stand up in front of others to speak. Or confront a loved one who may reject our message. Or follow through when God calls us to step out of our comfort zone. The truth is, we all feel insecure at times. We find ourselves wondering if we have what it takes to tackle the challenge that looms before us.

God understands. And that's why we see His words of encouragement throughout Scripture. He was and is calling a nervous lot to look to Him to strengthen our feeble arms and weak knees. Like Peter, we tend to get distracted by the waves all around us, and we take our eyes off the Savior. But with a good network of supporting friends to remind us of God's sufficiency, we can step forward in faith—even onto the water!

Energize the limp hands,
strengthen the rubbery knees.
Tell fearful souls,
"Courage! Take heart!
GOD is here, right here,
on His way to put things right
And redress all wrongs.
He's on his way! He'll save you!"

Isaiah 35:4 THE MESSAGE

Life-Giving Words for *Nervous Friends*

"This is the word of the LORD to Zerubbabel: 'Not by might nor by power, but by my Spirit,' says the LORD Almighty." ZECHARIAH 4:6 NIV

Take some pressure off yourself. It's not your intellect or ability that will make the difference. It's the presence and power of God's Spirit within you.

∞∞∞∞∞∞∞∞

"Don't worry about how you should defend yourselves or what you should say. For the Holy Spirit will teach you at that very hour what must be said." LUKE 12:11-12

Instead of stressing about what you're going to say, ask God for help. He has promised to give you the right words at the right time when you rely on His Spirit for guidance.

∞∞∞∞∞∞∞∞

Don't worry about anything, but in everything, through prayer and petition with thanksgiving, present your requests to God. And the peace of God, which surpasses all understanding, will guard your hearts and minds in Christ Jesus. PHILIPPIANS 4:6-7

Let your anxious thoughts switch to thankful words. A grateful heart shifts our focus from ourselves to God's greatness. He's got this!

∞∞∞∞∞∞∞∞

The LORD is for me; I will not be afraid. What can a mere mortal do to me? The LORD is my Helper, Therefore, I will look in triumph on those who hate me. PSALM 118:6-7

God is for you! What other approval do you really need?

*Do not fear, for I am with you; do not be afraid, for I am your God.
I will strengthen you; I will help you; I will hold on to you
with My righteous right hand.* ISAIAH 41:10

God's not going to loosen His grip on you. He loves you,
and you are totally secure in His hands.

✧✧✧✧✧✧✧✧✧

*I sought the LORD, and He answered me
and rescued me from all my fears.* PSALM 34:4

Let's ask Jesus to remove the fear and nervousness you're experiencing
right now and replace those feelings with His lasting peace.

✧✧✧✧✧✧✧✧✧

*Humble yourselves, therefore, under the mighty hand of God,
o that He may exalt you at the proper time, casting all your cares on Him,
because He cares about you.* I PETER 5:6-7

Nothing is too big or too small to bring before our Father.
Speak about your worries honestly, openly, and as often as you need.
Then leave them all with Him to handle.

✧✧✧✧✧✧✧✧✧

*"Can any of you add one moment to his life span by worrying?...So don't worry,
saying, 'What will we eat?' or 'What will we drink?' or 'What will we wear?'
For the Gentiles eagerly seek all these things, and your heavenly Father knows that
you need them. But seek first the kingdom of God and His righteousness, and all
these things will be provided for you."* MATTHEW 6:27, 31-33

When we fix our eyes on our Father, we become more
aware of His presence with us, His power, and the divine
peace He gives us. Our heavenly Father is an Awesome
Provider who has promised to meet our every need.

Words of Life for the
Insecure

She could see it on her daughter's face. In frustration, the teen slammed the brush down on the counter.

"What's the point?" she snarled. "No matter what I do, I'm still fat and ugly!" she shouted as she stormed off to her room. Clearly, she wasn't seeing the beautiful girl that not only her mother, but many others also saw. *How can her perception of herself be so off?* the mother wondered as she made her way to console her child.

If we asked, the mother would admit she suffers similar insecurities. Feelings of inadequacy and unworthiness simmer beneath a more sophisticated facade, surfacing only in her most vulnerable moments.

What do both mother and daughter need to know to set their souls free from this insecurity? How can we, as the body of Christ, encourage other believers struggling with insecurities? As always, our Savior shows us the way. His words of identity and belonging, beauty and purpose can tear through the masks we wear to work true healing where the deepest wounds lie. Let's point each other to our identity in Christ, our eternally secure identity as a beloved child of God.

Don't throw away
your confidence,
which has a
great reward.

Hebrews 10:35

Life-Giving Words for the *Insecure*

It is better to take refuge in the LORD than to trust in humanity. PSALM 118:8

People can't give us the self-confidence we crave.
God can, and He readily speaks of His great love for us.
May we find refuge in that love.

∞∞∞∞∞∞∞∞∞

There has never been the slightest doubt in my mind that the God who started this great work in you would keep at it and bring it to a flourishing finish on the very day Christ Jesus appears. PHILIPPIANS 1:6 THE MESSAGE

Relax! God is the One who started the grand work I see happening in you, and He's going to keep it going until you reach your full potential and are doing what He created you to do.

∞∞∞∞∞∞∞∞∞

This is the confidence we have before Him: If we ask anything according to His will, He hears us. I JOHN 5:14

You have the unwavering attention of the Creator of the universe.
What a source of confidence!

∞∞∞∞∞∞∞∞∞

I have been crucified with Christ, and I no longer live, but Christ lives in me. The life I now live in the body, I live by faith in the Son of God, who loved me and gave Himself for me. I do not set aside the grace of God, for if righteousness comes through the law, then Christ died for nothing GALATIANS 2:20-21

When we're at the center of our own universe, we suffocate.
Christ sets us free to find our worth, beauty, and purpose in Him.

74

You are no longer foreigners and strangers, but fellow citizens with the saints, and members of God's household EPHESIANS 2:19

Even while we still struggle with sin, God says we're saints. Jesus changes everything!

∞∞∞∞∞∞∞

"I have called you friends, because I have made known to you everything I have heard from My Father." JOHN 15:15

Jesus shares His heart with you because you are His friend— and He is yours.

∞∞∞∞∞∞∞

In [Jesus our Lord] we have boldness and confident access through faith in Him. EPHESIANS 3:12

There's no need to be shy with God. We are His kids! So climb into His lap and let Him know what you need.

∞∞∞∞∞∞∞

In [Jesus] we have redemption, the forgiveness of sins. COLOSSIANS 1:14

You can come out from hiding! Your sins are forgiven. Let God's favor fill you with joy.

∞∞∞∞∞∞∞

There is now no condemnation for those in Christ Jesus, because the law of the Spirit of life in Christ Jesus has set you free from the law of sin and death. ROMANS 8:1-2

Don't beat yourself up! Jesus took your guilt and shame with Him to the cross. One result of that grace is we are permanently fixed in our Father's affection.

Words of Life for the
Disappointed

The forecast called for a 100% chance of snow overnight. In the deep South, snow is rare, so the announcement sent everyone to the local grocery stores so they would be ready for the great winter storm. School was cancelled, businesses closed, and everyone waited.

And the storm arrived—but it left without leaving a trace of the promised winter glory. It was just another gray, wet, dismally cold day. What a disappointment!

Granted, in the world of letdowns, bad weather ranks pretty low on the list. But even such small events can sow seeds of a subtle-but-sinister skepticism. It's just *another* disappointment. *Another* indication that life doesn't work well. *Further* evidence that we can't trust that good is on its way. When we start listening to the enemy's lies, we find ourselves doubting God's goodness.

But disappointments don't have to lead us to despair. With we choose the right perspective, life's letdowns can actually usher in deeper trust in a God who doesn't act according to our plans, but whose purposes are far higher and better than our own.

When fellow believers face disappointment, we can walk alongside them and bear the load with them. Then, as the Spirit leads, we can speak words of life and hope that remind them of God's past faithfulness and His promise for a brighter future.

LORD, sustain me
as you promised,
that I may live!
Do not let my
hope be crushed.

Psalm 119:116 NLT

Life-Giving Words
for the *Disappointed*

"My thoughts are not your thoughts, and your ways are not My ways." This is the Lord's declaration. "For as heaven is higher than earth, so My ways are higher than your ways, and My thoughts than your thoughts." ISAIAH 55:8-9

Sometimes it's hard, if not impossible, to figure out why God does what He does. The only thing I know for sure is that He is good and He's in charge—so the best option is to just trust Him.

∞∞∞∞∞∞∞∞

[God's] anger lasts only a moment, but His favor, a lifetime. Weeping may stay overnight, but there is joy in the morning. PSALM 30:5

God loves to write comeback stories in our lives. Just when we think we're down for the count, our gracious God comes in for the rescue.

∞∞∞∞∞∞∞∞

We… rejoice in our afflictions, because we know that affliction produces endurance, endurance produces proven character, and proven character produces hope. This hope will not disappoint us, because God's love has been poured out in our hearts through the Holy Spirit who was given to us. ROMANS 5:3-5

Just as grapes must be crushed to release the juice within, God uses our disappointments to press us into Him. When we choose to trust Him in the often painful process, that trust is evidence that God is changing our character and making us more like Jesus.

∞∞∞∞∞∞∞∞

*Cast your burden on the Lord, and He will sustain you;
He will never allow the righteous to be shaken.* PSALM 55:22

Tell the Lord about all that discourages you. He listens with love and will lead you down a better path than you could have ever imagined.

Though the fig tree does not bud and there is no fruit on the vines, though the olive crop fails and the fields produce no food, though the flocks disappear from the pen and there are no herds in the stalls, yet I will celebrate in the LORD; I will rejoice in the God of my salvation! HABAKKUK 3:17-18

Great joy comes with worship. And it shouldn't surprise us that our disappointment fades as we remember how much God has given us in Jesus.

◇◇◇◇◇◇◇◇◇◇

He brought streams out of the stone and made water flow down like rivers. PSALM 78:16

If God can bring water out of stone, He can certainly carve a path for you around this obstacle. Pray for better vision so you're able to see His direction!

◇◇◇◇◇◇◇◇◇◇

Cast your burden on the LORD, and He will sustain you; He will never allow the righteous to be shaken. PSALM 55:22

Tell the Lord about all that discourages you. He listens with love and will lead you down a better path than you could have ever imagined.

◇◇◇◇◇◇◇◇◇◇

Wait for the LORD; be strong, and let your heart be courageous. Wait for the LORD. PSALM 27:14

Life's roadblocks can be so frustrating. But if God has called you to be on that road, He will open a way at just the right time. Wait and see!

Words of Life to
Bring Restoration

She was in trouble. Carelessly, in a conversation the day before, she'd let slip out something a friend had confided in her. And now that friend knows of the betrayed trust. That was clear the moment she sat down across the table. The confrontation was coming....

What do we say when we know we're guilty? When we've been called on the carpet by someone or we're feeling convicted by God Himself? Of course we want to find a way out. But denying our guilt—lying—is not a good option. God calls us to go a different direction.

When we've betrayed a friend, the path to restoration begins with an attitude of humility on our part and a solid belief that God forgives. As we understand our own depravity in light of our holy God's unrelenting grace, we gain the boldness to come clean, to admit our failures, and to honestly, authentically, ask those we offended to forgive us. As we confess our sins to God *and* to one another, God says we are healed. We have no need to hide or pretend, and can choose to walk a better way next time.

"If you are offering your gift
at the altar and there remember
that your brother or sister
has something against you,
leave your gift there in front
of the altar. First go and
be reconciled to them;
then come and offer your gift."

Matthew 5:23-24 NIV

Life-Giving Words to
Bring Restoration

I acknowledged my sin to You and did not conceal my iniquity.
I said, "I will confess my transgressions to the LORD,"
and You forgave the guilt of my sin. PSALM 32:5

I'm tired of pretending I'm right. It's time for me to come clean.

⸱⸱⸱⸱⸱⸱⸱⸱⸱⸱⸱⸱

I confess my iniquity; I am anxious because of my sin. PSALM 38:18

Something has been eating me alive, and I need to be
completely honest with you. Can we talk?

⸱⸱⸱⸱⸱⸱⸱⸱⸱⸱⸱⸱

The one who conceals his sins will not prosper, but whoever confesses
and renounces them will find mercy. PROVERBS 28:13

It was completely wrong for me to respond to you the way I did.
I can see that I hurt you, and I'd like to try to make it right.

⸱⸱⸱⸱⸱⸱⸱⸱⸱⸱⸱⸱

Who perceives his unintentional sins?
Cleanse me from my hidden faults. PSALM 19:12

You've seemed distant lately. Have I done something
or said anything that offended you?

⸱⸱⸱⸱⸱⸱⸱⸱⸱⸱⸱⸱

Confess your sins to one another and pray for one another, so that you may be
healed. The prayer of a righteous person is very powerful in its effect. JAMES 5:16

I can't seem to overcome this sin in my life. No matter how hard I try,
I keep failing. Would you please hold me accountable
in this area and pray for my victory?

If we walk in the light as [God] Himself is in the light, we have fellowship with one another, and the blood of Jesus His Son cleanses us from all sin. I JOHN 1:7

It feels like there is a wall between us whenever we talk.
I'd love for that wall to come down. What can I do differently
to help you feel safe to talk to me?

❦

*If we say, "We have no sin," we are deceiving ourselves,
and the truth is not in us.* I JOHN 1:8

When you confronted me, I know I got defensive.
But the truth is, I know you were right; God confirmed it in my spirit.
I was wrong. Will you forgive me?

❦

*God, You know my foolishness, and my guilty acts
are not hidden from You.* PSALM 69:5

God, I know you saw me when I _____.
Please forgive me and help me to draw strength from Your Spirit
so I can say no to the next temptation.

❦

*If I had been aware of malice in my heart,
the Lord would not have listened.* PSALM 66:18

Lord, I know You hear my critical thoughts as loudly as You do my
words. I want both my thoughts and my words to better honor You.
Please forgive me and heal my heart.

Words of Life That
Give Grace

He did it. Again. He'd promised to pay that bill when the money came in, but he unthinkingly spent it on something else. Now you're holding the overdue notice in your hand with no way to pay it—and to say that you're angry is a huge understatement. The repeated offense makes you want to scream, get in his face, vent all your frustration and fear.

But, first, consider the lasting effects. Once we speak, we can't recover or unsay our words. Our anger can wreak havoc far worse than the wrong that inspired it. Instead of a tirade, we need a prayer. We need to seek our Savior and ask for His help in applying to our current situation His amazing grace that saved us from an eternity in hell. Let's ask His Spirit to supply us with the right words of life—words that acknowledge the situation, address the pain, and place the hope for restoration in the hands of the Healer.

Our help comes from the Lord, not in how well the object of our anger feels our wrath or grovels to get out of it. When we see the Lord as sufficient in our time of need, we can pour out words of life-giving grace instead.

Above all, maintain
constant love
for one another,
since love covers
a multitude of sins.

I Peter 4:8

Life-Giving Words
that *Give Grace*

*The LORD God is our sun and our shield. He gives us grace and glory. The LORD
will withhold no good thing from those who do what is right.* PSALM 84:11 NLT

God has protected me and promised to take care of me.
You hurt me, but I forgive you.

○○○○○○○○○○○○

*A person's insight gives him patience,
and his virtue is to overlook an offense.* PROVERBS 19:11

That's OK. Let's just try this again another way.

○○○○○○○○○○○○

*To all who are in Rome, loved by God, called as saints. Grace to you and peace
from God our Father and the Lord Jesus Christ.* ROMANS 1:7

Father, fill me with Your grace and peace as I plan to release
this person from the debt they owe me.

○○○○○○○○○○○○

*By the grace of God I am what I am, and His grace toward me was not in vain.
On the contrary, I worked harder than any of them, yet not I,
but the grace of God that was with me.* I CORINTHIANS 15:10

God has given me a soft heart about your situation.
What can I do to help you?

○○○○○○○○○○○○

*All have sinned and fall short of the glory of God. They are justified freely by
His grace through the redemption that is in Christ Jesus.* ROMANS 3:23-24

Given the same circumstances, I might have done
the same thing. I forgive you.

The Word became flesh and dwelt among us. We observed His glory, the glory as the one and only Son from the Father, full of grace and truth. JOHN 1:14

Jesus was full of grace and truth. Since His Spirit is in me, I want to extend grace to you in this matter.

<hr />

Through [Jesus] we have received grace and apostleship to bring about the obedience of faith for the sake of His name among all the Gentiles. ROMANS 1:5

My faith doesn't mean anything if I don't apply it, especially in the area of forgiveness. In obedience to the Lord, I'm choosing to overlook this offense.

<hr />

May grace and peace be multiplied to you through the knowledge of God and of Jesus our Lord. II PETER 1:2

I hope that my actions help you see Jesus a little more clearly and understand His grace and love a little more.

<hr />

Just as each one has received a gift, use it to serve others, as good stewards of the varied grace of God. I PETER 4:10

God has gifted me with His grace in this area so that I can be a blessing, even in the difficult circumstances.

<hr />

By the grace given to me, I tell everyone among you not to think of himself more highly than he should think. Instead, think sensibly, as God has distributed a measure of faith to each one. ROMANS 12:3

I'm trusting God to take care of the situation, despite the mistake that was made. He may even use that oversight to point us in a better direction!

Words of Life for
Enduring Trials

Every time the coach whistled to send in another substitute instead of her son, the mom felt her frustration growing into a volcano that was certain to blow any second.

Why doesn't the coach see his potential? Why is he wasting all our time?! Doesn't he know how humiliating it is to stay seated on the bench? She was seething. It was all she could do to stay seated instead of marching out onto the field to give that coach a piece of her mind.

But then God gave her a peace of His own mind and heart. *Is there any better way for your son to learn patience, trust, and humility than on that lonely, lowly bench?* God asked her spirit.

And she realized the truth. Trials take us to a fork in the road: Will we protest the path and part ways with God, or will we simply trust Him? Will we seek to establish control of our own, or will we yield to His plan? When we ourselves encounter difficulty or when we see our loved ones suffering, it's tempting to focus on the circumstances and to fight our way out of them. But this is the moment when we most need to pray, asking God for His wisdom and perspective. In these moments, we can use our words to urge others down the right path or the wrong one. In the midst of the trials, let's focus on Jesus, the Author and Perfecter of our faith.

[Human fathers]
disciplined us for a
short time based on what
seemed good to them,
but [our heavenly Father]
does it for our benefit,
so that we can share
His holiness.

Hebrews 12:10

Life-Giving Words for *Enduring Trials*

*We are afflicted in every way but not crushed; we are perplexed
but not in despair; we are persecuted but not abandoned;
we are struck down but not destroyed.* II Corinthians 4:8-9

What you are enduring is difficult,
but God will not let you be crushed.

<hr>

*Look, I have refined you, but not as silver; I have tested you
in the furnace of affliction.* Isaiah 48:10

God is doing a painful but beautiful work in you
to make you more like Jesus.

<hr>

*I know both how to make do with little, and I know how to make do with a lot.
In any and all circumstances I have learned the secret of being content—
whether well fed or hungry, whether in abundance or in need. I am able to do
all things through Him who strengthens me.* Philippians 4:12-13

Our circumstances don't determine our success. Our Savior does.

<hr>

*Consider it a great joy, my brothers and sisters, whenever you experience
various trials, because you know that the testing of your faith
produces endurance. And let endurance have its full effect,
so that you may be mature and complete, lacking nothing* James 1:2-4

God is growing you up so that you not only experience His comfort,
but you are also equipped to comfort others.

Be sober-minded, be alert. Your adversary the devil is prowling around like a roaring lion, looking for anyone he can devour. Resist him, firm in the faith, knowing that the same kind of sufferings are being experienced by your fellow believers throughout the world. I Peter 5:8-9

You are not alone in your suffering. Brothers and sisters around the world struggle. Know I'm standing with you.

∞∞∞∞∞∞∞∞

Rejoice as you share in the sufferings of Christ, so that you may also rejoice with great joy when His glory is revealed. I Peter 4:13

God works His sovereign and loving plan through suffering. As we walk through it with faith as our Savior did, we grow to be more like Him.

∞∞∞∞∞∞∞∞

As for you, be strong; don't give up, for your work has a reward. II Chronicles 15:7

The only way you can fail is if you give up. Keep trusting the Lord and watch what He will do.

∞∞∞∞∞∞∞∞

Do not be conformed to this age, but be transformed by the renewing of your mind, so that you may discern what is the good, pleasing, and perfect will of God. Romans 12:2

Don't look at your circumstances the way the world does. Know that God loves you, and He has allowed this experience in order to grow your reliance on Him.

Words of Life That
Create Unity

The new district manager had just ended the first
conference call with his team. By his standards, this initial
interaction with the sales reps he now managed seemed to go
pretty well. But when he left the call, the team blasted him:
"Can you believe he's changing everything around like that?
We were doing just fine before he got here" and "You know
how he got the position, don't you? Don't say I said it, but...."
The toxic dissension spread throughout the team like gangrene
until everyone, even the silent listeners, felt sick.

And so it is when we allow the enemy, or even each other sow
divisive thoughts into our lives. Hostility and division leads
to the death of our relationships at work and at home, in our
neighborhoods and churches, via social media, and throughout
the culture at large.

Our enemy turns us against each other and keeps us from
fulfilling our God-given purpose on this planet: to love Him
and the people He made with all we are. But we can fight
Satan's schemes. When we counter gossip and division with
wise words that unite, we invite others into peace and unity—
into God's purpose—in each situation.

There is no
Jew or Greek,
slave or free,
male and female;
since you are all
one in Christ Jesus.

Galatians 3:28

Life-Giving Words That *Create Unity*

*Whoever conceals an offense promotes love,
but whoever gossips about it separates friends.* PROVERBS 17:9

I know you wanted to retaliate after what he did to you,
but you showed incredible restraint instead. Good job!

<hr/>

*No foul language should come from your mouth, but only what is good for building
up someone in need, so that it gives grace to those who hear.* EPHESIANS 4:29

I am so thankful I get to work with people like you. You are awesome!

<hr/>

*Watch out for those who create divisions and obstacles contrary to the teaching
that you learned. Avoid them, because such people do not serve our Lord Christ
but their own appetites. They deceive the hearts of the unsuspecting
with smooth talk and flattering words.* ROMANS 16:17-18

I'm sorry your friendship is going through a rough patch.
But talking about it to everyone else won't help you
nearly as much as taking the matter directly to her/him.

<hr/>

*I urge you, brothers and sisters, in the name of our Lord Jesus Christ,
that all of you agree in what you say, that there be no divisions
among you, and that you be united with the same understanding
and the same conviction.* I CORINTHIANS 1:10

No matter our denomination, all of us who trust Jesus
for salvation belong to Him. Let's find ways
to work together to build His kingdom!

Don't all of us have one Father? Didn't one God create us?
Why then do we act treacherously against one another,
profaning the covenant of our fathers? MALACHI 2:10

When you got married, God joined you two together as one. So don't
let anyone or anything come between you. Fight for your family!

<hr />

"You are not to be called 'Rabbi,' because you have one Teacher,
and you are all brothers and sisters. Do not call anyone on earth your father,
because you have one Father, who is in heaven." MATTHEW 23:8-9

Our Father loves us, His children. And like any good parent,
He wants us to love one another more than
He wants us to prove we are right.

<hr />

You are a holy people belonging to the LORD your God.
The LORD your God has chosen you to be His own possession out
of all the peoples on the face of the earth. DEUTERONOMY 7:6

In this dark world, we are set apart to shine forth the glory
of God that He shines on His people. Let's not allow division
to destroy our reflection of His glory and love!

<hr />

[By faith, Moses] chose to suffer with the people of God rather than
to enjoy the fleeting pleasure of sin. HEBREWS 11:25

Thank you for always reminding us to trust God and obey even
when we don't fully understand all the details.
Your eternal perspective always reminds us to make
good choices and stand on His promises.

Words of Life That
Win Spiritual Wars

The servant was terrified. When he awoke from his night's sleep and looked outside the window, he saw that the enemy army had completely surrounded the city with the sole purpose of taking down his master, the prophet Elisha.

"What should we do?" the panicked servant asked Elisha.

In response, the prophet simply prayed, "Lord, open his eyes."

Suddenly, the servant saw another much larger, and clearly more powerful, army of angel warriors surrounding and protecting Elisha and him. The servant's fear gave way to wonder at God's power.

You and I can suffer from the same kind of blindness that afflicted Elisha's servant. We easily see the people around us and the circumstances of life as the reason for our struggles. But, as the Bible tells us, the real enemies are unseen spiritual forces of evil (Ephesians 6:11-12).

It's critical that we learn to see God's unseen forces of good. May we cooperate with our Lord who has the power to open our eyes to see and our minds to understand the real enemy we are up against. May we also rely on the incredible power we have to fight back with God's Word and the indwelling Holy Spirit. And let us help one other see beneath the surface to the deeper spiritual issues at play. Then may we press into Jesus, our Commander and Lord, who leads us into certain victory.

They conquered
him by the blood
of the Lamb
and by the word
of their testimony.

Revelation 12:11

Life-Giving Words That *Win Spiritual Wars*

Submit to God. Resist the devil, and he will flee from you. JAMES 4:7

God gives you the power to say no to the enemy and yes to His Spirit.
So resist the devil, obey God, and by His grace, stand in victory!

<hr>

*Although we live in the flesh, we do not wage war according to the flesh,
since the weapons of our warfare are not of the flesh, but are powerful
through God for the demolition of strongholds. We demolish arguments
and every proud thing that is raised up against the knowledge of God, and we
take every thought captive to obey Christ.* II CORINTHIANS 10:3-5

Our enemy—Satan himself—twists the truth and causes division.
Together, let's address the lies head on and trust God's Word instead.

<hr>

*You are from God, little children, and you have conquered
[spirits that do not confess Jesus}, because the One who is in you
is greater than the one who is in the world.* I JOHN 4:4

This spiritual battle may seem impossible, but God is greater than
this—and any—problem. He will help you fight to the victory!

<hr>

*"No weapon formed against you will succeed, and you will refute any accusation
raised against you in court. This is the heritage of the Lord's servants, and their
vindication is from Me." This is the LORD's declaration.* ISAIAH 54:17

The enemy may be using that person to spread all kinds of lies
about you, but God will bring your vindication.
So keep your eyes on Him and your conscience clear!

Our struggle is not against flesh and blood, but against the rulers, against the authorities, against the cosmic powers of this darkness, against evil, spiritual forces in the heavens. For this reason take up the full armor of God, so that you may be able to resist in the evil day, and having prepared everything, to take your stand. EPHESIANS 6:12-13

Remember that Jesus both surrounds you and provides you with supernatural armor. So take up your shield of faith and hold it up when the enemy's missiles fly!

◇◇◇◇◇◇◇◇◇◇◇

Pray at all times in the Spirit with every prayer and request, and stay alert with all perseverance and intercession for all the saints. EPHESIANS 6:18

Lord, right now I'm asking You to help _____.
Please bless her/him with a real sense of Your presence,
fill her/him with Your Spirit, and guide her/his steps.

◇◇◇◇◇◇◇◇◇◇◇

No, in all these things [affliction or distress or persecution or famine or nakedness or danger or sword] we are more than conquerors through Him who loved us. ROMANS 8:37

God forgives us, but He doesn't stop there. He grants us full access to every spiritual blessing so that we'll be able to do better next time.

◇◇◇◇◇◇◇◇◇◇◇

The Lord is faithful; he will strengthen and guard you from the evil one. II THESSALONIANS 3:3

You never fight a battle alone. Your Lord, the Commander of heaven's armies, fights with you, interceding for you before the Father and strengthening you by His Spirit.

Words of Life for Those
Who Are Angry

It's hard to be on social media and not encounter angry people. Just open up almost any forum, and you can find people furious with people whose faces they've never even seen. No matter the topic, people take polar opposite extremes and viciously attack opposing positions with words you'd never want your kids to hear. The hatred is deep and dark.

Proverbs says that fools give full vent to their anger. Without any hint of restraint, these individuals allow all the evil inside to come flowing out of their mouths. But Romans 2:4 says the kindness of the Lord leads us to repentance. In Christ, we find it possible to speak truth and share opinions with gentleness and kindness, confident that God's Spirit (rather than the effectiveness of our argument) will produce the change we want to see.

If we want to create a culture of peace and kindness, let's start with repenting for the harmful words we've spoken in our home, workplace, and relationships or posted on social media. After confessing our sin and receiving God's forgiveness, we can ask God's Spirit to help us show restraint in the heat of the moment and to give us wisdom so, at the right time, we speak calming, gentle, and powerful words of truth in humility and love.

Everyone should
be quick to listen,
slow to speak,
and slow to anger,
for human anger
does not accomplish
God's righteousness.

James 1:19-20

Life-Giving Words for Those *Who Are Angry*

Be angry and do not sin. Don't let the sun go down on your anger. EPHESIANS 4:26

I know we both feel the tension. Know that I'd love to calmly talk this out with you. I don't want this misunderstanding to come between us and fracture this relationship.

<hr>

Be angry and do not sin; on your bed, reflect in your heart and be still. PSALM 4:4

Lord, I know that I'm angry, but I'm not exactly sure why. Will you please reveal the root cause so that I can bring it to You and let go?

<hr>

A person's insight gives him patience, and his virtue is to overlook an offense. PROVERBS 19:11

I understand why you're angry. I've actually been in a similar situation before. Let's work together toward a solution that's better for both of us.

<hr>

A gentle answer turns away anger, but a harsh word stirs up wrath. PROVERBS 15:1

I can see that you're upset. What can I do to help you right now?

<hr>

"Just as you want others to do for you, do the same for them." LUKE 6:31

Thank you for treating me with respect even after I blew up at you.

Refrain from anger and give up your rage;
do not be agitated—it can only bring harm. PSALM 37:8

Lord, help me to walk away from this argument right now
before I say something I regret and dishonor You.

∞∞∞∞∞∞∞∞∞

Put away all the following: anger, wrath, malice, slander, and filthy language
from your mouth…. Put on compassion, kindness, humility, gentleness,
and patience, bearing with one another and forgiving one another if anyone
has a grievance against another. COLOSSIANS 3:8, 12-13

Even though we disagree and even fight sometimes,
I want you to know that I care deeply about you.
I regularly pray for God to bless you and your family.

∞∞∞∞∞∞∞∞∞

"Do not judge, and you will not be judged. Do not condemn, and you will
not be condemned. Forgive, and you will be forgiven." LUKE 6:37

I've noticed that when everyone else posted critical
and rude arguments online, your comments were positive
and insightful. Good job!

∞∞∞∞∞∞∞∞∞

Do not be conquered by evil, but conquer evil with good. ROMANS 12:21

I'm sorry that you feel that way, but I wish you the best.

∞∞∞∞∞∞∞∞∞

Love one another deeply as brothers and sisters. Outdo one another
in showing honor. ROMANS 12:10

Thank you for finding the courage to share that with me.
Wounds from a friend are truly better than kisses
from an enemy. Your honesty, while hard to hear,
will help me be a better person.

Words of Life That
Build Identity

She thought she had weathered the transition quite well.
She had figured that after they sent their last son off to college,
she'd finally get to all those projects she had put off in busier
years. But she hadn't expected the onslaught of emotions
that hit her in her children's absence. Knowing that everyone
experiences midlife crises in some way didn't satisfy the
nagging void in her life. Her mothering season was over. *What
do I do now?* she wondered. *For that matter, who am I now?*

Empty nesters aren't the only ones asking these questions. The
search for significance and identity fuels human behavior in
a myriad of ways. Many of us try to prove our value through
our efforts at the office, raising kids, and achieving a desired
degree of success or fame.

But our Father fashioned us for a bigger purpose: He created
us to know Him and be in relationship with Him as part of His
family. Ideally, all the activities, roles, and responsibilities we
undertake in this life will flow from this central truth, providing
us with an unshakable and unchanging identity in Jesus. When
our loved ones are reeling from change, let's remind them
whose they are and who they will always be: God's dearly loved
children. And may we remember this truth ourselves.

"I have called
you by your name;
you are Mine."

Isaiah 43:1

Life-Giving Words
That *Build Identity*

To all who did receive [Jesus], He gave them the right to be children of God, to those who believe in His name. JOHN 1:12

You are God's son/daughter whom He dearly loves!

⁕⁕⁕⁕⁕⁕⁕⁕⁕⁕

Anyone joined to the Lord is one spirit with Him. I CORINTHIANS 6:17

The Father welcomes you to ask Him for whatever you need.

⁕⁕⁕⁕⁕⁕⁕⁕⁕⁕

So God created man in His own image; He created him in the image of God; He created them male and female. GENESIS 1:27

It doesn't matter how old and wrinkled we get,
we will still bear the image of God! In fact, some of those traits
may be even more striking then!

⁕⁕⁕⁕⁕⁕⁕⁕⁕⁕

I [the Lord] chose you [Jeremiah] before I formed you in the womb; I set you apart before you were born. I appointed you a prophet to the nations. JEREMIAH 1:5

God established this season of your life for a purpose.
Ask Him what that purpose is, listen quietly at His feet,
and then follow His instructions.

⁕⁕⁕⁕⁕⁕⁕⁕⁕⁕

If anyone is in Christ, he is a new creation; the old has passed away, and see, the new has come! II CORINTHIANS 5:17

No longer are you that person you once were. You are brand-new,
filled with God's Spirit, empowered to obey and to glorify God.

You are a chosen race, a royal priesthood, a holy nation, a people for His possession, so that you may proclaim the praises of the One who called you out of darkness into His marvelous light. I PETER 2:9

I know what you did in the past, but that's not who you are. You are a Christ-follower, chosen by God, who still struggles with sin... as all of us do. Repent and return to your calling! God will take you back.

∞∞∞∞∞∞∞∞∞∞

See what great love the Father has given us that we should be called God's children—and we are! The reason the world does not know us is that it didn't know Him. Dear friends, we are God's children now, and what we will be has not yet been revealed. We know that when He appears, we will be like Him because we will see Him as He is. I JOHN 3:1-2

I see Jesus in you. You are an encouragement to me!

∞∞∞∞∞∞∞∞∞∞

If you have been raised with Christ, seek the things above, where Christ is, seated at the right hand of God. Set your minds on things above, not on earthly things. For you died, and your life is hidden with Christ in God. COLOSSIANS 3:1-3

Lord, please teach me to set my mind on heavenly things and divine truths. In doing so, may I learn to see this world from Your vantage point.

∞∞∞∞∞∞∞∞∞∞

"I am the vine; you are the branches. The one who remains in Me and I in him produces much fruit, because you can do nothing without Me." JOHN 15:5

When you walk close to Jesus, He makes every moment of your life fruitful.

Words of Life That
Build Faith

Her face full of anger, the young teen told her Bible study small group, *My mom and dad are getting a divorce.* But as she explained a little more, her strong facade cracked, and tears trickled down her face. *Where is the Lord now?*

She asked, desperate for an answer. *Why isn't He doing anything to stop this?*

It's easy to talk about faith and trust when life is pretty good. But when something happens that rocks our world, we ask a lot of questions about our faith: *Is God really in control? Is He really good? Does He care at all about me?*

Doubts fill our minds and threaten to snap the connection with God we thought was so strong. Satan loves to visit at these moments of weakness, and his goal is to keep us mired in our despair until our faith dies altogether.

But our God is stronger than evil, and His love is great enough to buoy any floundering faith. When we're in life's trenches, we need to remind each other of our Almighty God—of His character, His past faithfulness, of the gospel truth. As we lift each other up, setting our gazes on God's immutable character, we remember just how mighty He is to save.

Faith is the
reality of what
is hoped for,
the proof of
what is not seen.

Hebrews 11:1

Life-Giving Words
That *Build Faith*

We walk by faith, not by sight. II CORINTHIANS 5:7

Even though a given situation doesn't make sense to the watching
world or even to us who follow Jesus, God is working out a plan so
great and glorious we can't even imagine it. But we can trust Him!

∞∞∞∞∞∞∞∞

The father of the boy cried out, "I do believe; help my unbelief!" MARK 9:24

There's no need to cover up your fears and doubts because God
already knows them anyway. Just ask Him to help you believe,
and He'll graciously give you the faith you need.

∞∞∞∞∞∞∞∞

*Without faith it is impossible to please God, since the one who
draws near to Him must believe that He exists and that
He rewards those who seek Him.* HEBREWS 11:6

Don't give up seeking the Lord. He promises to reward us when
we continue to press in to know and understand His heart.

∞∞∞∞∞∞∞∞

*My speech and my preaching were not with persuasive words of wisdom but with
a demonstration of the Spirit's power, so that your faith might not be based on
human wisdom but on God's power.* I CORINTHIANS 2:4-5

When you spoke up today and shared from your heart,
I really heard the Lord speaking to me through you.
Thank you for being vulnerable.

*Faith comes from what is heard, and what is heard comes through
the message about Christ.* ROMANS 10:17

I love the way you rely on Scripture to inform your decisions
and shape your opinions. You have wisdom beyond your years.

◇◇◇◇◇◇◇◇◇◇◇◇

*You are saved by grace through faith, and this is not from yourselves;
it is God's gift—not from works, so that no one can boast.* EPHESIANS 2:8-9

Our salvation started by faith, and it continues and ends that way.
God invites you to rest in His provision!

◇◇◇◇◇◇◇◇◇◇◇◇

"If you believe, you will receive whatever you ask for in prayer." MATTHEW 21:22

I'm believing with you that God will provide the resources we need,
the resources we asked Him for.

◇◇◇◇◇◇◇◇◇◇◇◇

*A person is justified by works and not by faith alone…. For just as the body
without the spirit is dead, so also faith without works is dead.* JAMES 2:24, 26

I love the way you don't just talk about your faith. You live it out
by loving others so well. Everyone can see Jesus' love in you.

◇◇◇◇◇◇◇◇◇◇◇◇

*I have fought the good fight, I have finished the race,
I have kept the faith.* II TIMOTHY 4:7

God's Word says it's a fight to the finish, but we have a
reward waiting for us if we persevere. So keep believing
Jesus, because He never fails, and our reward is certain.

Words of Life for the
Rejected

Her jaw dropped when she first saw the picture her friends—her *close* friends—had posted. All of them were together. All of them were having what looked to be a wonderful time at the beach. But no one had invited her. She hadn't heard anything about it… until now. And she felt that familiar stabbing pain. This fresh rejection reiterated an all-too-familiar theme in her life: *You're not loved.*

The wounds of rejection cut far deeper than any knife can. Rejection goes right to our core and removes the hope that we have any worth, that we bring any value to this world, that we are wanted.

And rejection is a weapon of choice for the spiritual forces of darkness that seek our despair and ultimate doom. As long as we believe we aren't loved or wanted, we stay blind to that beautiful truth that God treasures us and wants to walk with us every moment of our lives! Our Creator God delights in His people so much that He never leaves us alone—and He never leaves us out. As members of God's family, we have the duty and privilege of reminding each other of the incredible reality that we are forever loved and accepted by our heavenly Father.

The LORD
will not leave
His people
or abandon
His heritage.

Psalm 94:14

Life-Giving Words for the *Rejected*

I have loved you with an everlasting love; therefore, I have continued to extend faithful love to you. JEREMIAH 31:3

Your Father sees your hurt and is holding you close.
His love will never fail you.

<><><><><><><>

If God is for us, who is against us? ROMANS 8:31

Life is hard, but know that God is not punishing you.
Instead, think of it as God pushing you to recognize
His presence with you in a new way.

<><><><><><><>

As you come to [Jesus], a living stone—rejected by people but chosen and honored by God—you yourselves, as living stones, a spiritual house, are being built to be a holy priesthood to offer spiritual sacrifices acceptable to God through Jesus Christ. I PETER 2:4-5

Don't isolate. Don't be a loner. God made you
to be a building block, a special part of the glorious
temple God is building. You belong here!

<><><><><><><>

The stone that the builders rejected has become the cornerstone. PSALM 118:22

Jesus experienced an excruciatingly painful rejection, and He did
so to pave the way for a glorious future. I'm praying that God
will not only ease the sting of rejection, but also provide
opportunities for you to make even better friends.

"If the world hates you, understand that it hated Me before it hated you." JOHN 15:18

Don't take personally the world's hatred and disdain. Darkness has always hated light, and the world is actually rejecting God, not you.

∞∞∞∞∞∞∞∞

Even if my father and mother abandon me, the LORD cares for me. PSALM 27:10

I am so sorry your parents responded that way. I can only imagine how much their rejection hurts. I hope you find comfort in the truths that your heavenly Father deeply loves you and that nothing can ever separate you from His love.

∞∞∞∞∞∞∞∞

Even my friend in whom I trusted, one who ate my bread, has raised his heel against me. But you, LORD, be gracious to me and raise me up. PSALM 41:9-10

We expect better behavior from believers, and that expectation can mean bigger disappointments and greater hurts when fellow Christians show they are still very much human. When a Christian wounds you, remember the grace God extended when He forgave you, and ask His help to forgive your brother or sister in the Lord. Go to your gracious God for the healing your heart needs.

∞∞∞∞∞∞∞∞

[Jesus] came to His own, and His own people did not receive Him. JOHN 1:11

Jesus knows exactly what it feels like to be rejected by people who should have loved Him. Let Him comfort you like no one else can.

Words of Life for When
We Need Guidance

She could hardly hear the words her professor spoke. Oh, she needed to know the material for the test, but her mind was elsewhere. Her heart was in tangles as she tossed the pros and cons of the budding relationship with the young man she met last semester. He was cute, sweet, and clearly in love with her. Compared to the lost causes she had dated before, he was an excellent choice. The decision really was a no-brainer, except….

Why shouldn't I pursue a relationship with him? she wondered. Yet she couldn't ignore the hesitation she sensed in her spirit. *Am I afraid of commitment? I don't think so. Of being hurt again? Of course… But maybe God's Spirit is protecting me from something I can't see.*

Like all of us, the young girl needed wisdom from above that takes into consideration more than a list of facts. We believers want to know what God wants for our lives, and then we'll move confidently in that direction. But how can we know when He doesn't spell it out in the sky for us? The uncertainty can sap our mental and emotional energy. We can feel like God isn't even speaking.

But He is. And He often speaks through His people. Maybe God has sent someone to you to remind you of something in His Word, something that you truly needed to hear right then. Or maybe God has enabled you to be that someone in another person's life.

Trust in the Lord
with all your heart,
and do not rely on your
own understanding;
in all your ways know Him,
and He will make
your paths straight.

Proverbs 3:5-6

Life-Giving Words for When *We Need Guidance*

Wait for the LORD; be strong, and let your heart be courageous.
Wait for the LORD. PSALM 27:14

No one likes to wait, but like all of God's commands,
this one is for our good. I'll wait with you until you have a better
understanding of what the Lord is going to do. His plans for you
are good. Wait for Him to reveal them.

∞∞∞∞∞∞∞∞∞∞

No temptation has come upon you except what is common to humanity.
But God is faithful; He will not allow you to be tempted beyond what
you are able, but with the temptation He will also provide a way out
so that you may be able to bear it. I CORINTHIANS 10:13

You are not a victim because of a past sin and therefore destined
to failure. You are victorious over sin because Jesus paid that price,
and you are very blessed because your God is with you. He will
provide a way out whenever you face temptation. Look for it!

∞∞∞∞∞∞∞∞∞∞

Seek the LORD and His strength; seek His face always. I CHRONICLES 16:11

Never stop seeking the Lord. Pursue Him daily, find strength in His
Word, guidance through prayer, and peace in His presence with you.

∞∞∞∞∞∞∞∞∞∞

I always let the LORD guide me. Because He is at my right hand,
I will not be shaken. PSALM 16:8

When you trust and rely on the Lord to lead you,
you can see Him redeem even worst of disasters.
In His time, He works everything out for your good.

118

Keep your life free from the love of money. Be satisfied with what you have, for He Himself has said, I will never leave you or abandon you. HEBREWS 13:5

When we need to make a decision, money is a very unreliable guide. That's undoubtedly one reason God warns us not to love and pursue money. So seek God's kingdom and His guidance first. Then watch Him direct your steps and provide all you need.

⬦⬦⬦⬦⬦⬦⬦⬦⬦⬦⬦

Search me, God, and know my heart; test me and know my concerns. See if there is any offensive way in me; lead me in the everlasting way. PSALM 139:23-24

Sometimes sin keeps us from hearing God speak. Ask Him to search you and cleanse you so that sin won't keep you from hearing from His Spirit.

⬦⬦⬦⬦⬦⬦⬦⬦⬦⬦⬦

Are inanimate objects your teachers? Look, it may be covered in gold and silver, But there is no breath of life inside. HABAKKUK 2:19 VOICE

Our culture might look to the stars or charms for signs and direction, but not God's people! We have a God in heaven who is very much alive, and He hears us and helps us whenever we call to Him!

⬦⬦⬦⬦⬦⬦⬦⬦⬦⬦⬦

Whenever you turn to the right or to the left, your ears will hear this command behind you: "This is the way. Walk in it." ISAIAH 30:21

Don't be afraid to take a step of faith. If you need to alter your direction after you do so, you'll hear God's Spirit tell you where to go from there.

Words of Life to
Bring Healing

The centurion we meet in Matthew 8 was a man of authority whom no one questioned and everyone obeyed. When he gave his subordinates orders, they acted immediately and with care.

So when the centurion approached Jesus for help, he understood a principle that people crowding around Him had missed. This Roman soldier knew that Jesus had far more authority than the highest ranking military official on earth, that Jesus commands the armies of heaven and controls the entire universe. When Jesus agreed to heal his servant, the centurion saved Him the trip to his home. "I am not worthy to have you come under my roof. But just say the word, and my servant will be healed" (Matthew 8:8). Jesus was amazed by the centurion's faith.

Throughout Scripture, we can learn about God's healing power. We learn, for instance, that He heals both physical and emotional wounds. We see that we don't have to muster up strength or find solutions on our own. Like the centurion, we need to see our Savior as sovereign over our situation; we need to recognize Jesus' power and authority over every obstacle we face in our lives.

Our God is mighty to save, and He is our Healer in every way. Let's look to the Great Physician to say the Word our lives and hearts need to hear. Today just may be the day He heals us.

The tongue of the wise brings healing.

Proverbs 12:18

Life-Giving Words to *Bring Healing*

Don't be wise in your own eyes; fear the LORD and turn away from evil. This will be healing for your body and strengthening for your bones. PROVERBS 3:7-8

God brings healing to our souls when we see Him alone as the Source of Hope.

◇◇◇◇◇◇◇◇◇◇◇◇

"If My people, who are called by My name, will humble themselves and pray and seek My face and turn from their wicked ways, then I will hear from heaven, and I will forgive their sin and will heal their land." II CHRONICLES 7:14 NIV

Repentance and healing always go hand in hand. Humbly ask God to reveal your sin, forgive your sin, and restore your soul. Then the stage is set for Him to heal your woundedness.

◇◇◇◇◇◇◇◇◇◇◇◇

"I have seen his ways, but I will heal him; I will lead him and restore comfort to him and his mourners, creating words of praise." ISAIAH 57:18-19

God doesn't treat us as our sins deserve. Holy and pure, God knows all too well the depths and darkness of our hearts, but He loves us and heals us anyway.

◇◇◇◇◇◇◇◇◇◇◇◇

How priceless Your faithful love is, God! People take refuge in the shadow of Your wings. They are filled from the abundance of Your house. You let them drink from Your refreshing stream. For the wellspring of life is with You. By means of Your light we see light. PSALM 36:7-9

God is our wellspring of life. Sit in His Presence and be refreshed by His Spirit in you.

Pleasant words are a honeycomb: sweet to the taste and health to the body.
PROVERBS 16:24

Your words of encouragement this morning healed my hurting heart.
Thank you for speaking up.

◇◇◇◇◇◇◇◇◇◇

Restore us, God; make your face shine on us, so that we may be saved. PSALM 80:3

God longs to shine His face toward us, but sometimes
we have to turn around to see it!

◇◇◇◇◇◇◇◇◇◇

*Oh, that Israel's deliverance would come from Zion! When the Lord restores the
fortunes of his people, let Jacob rejoice, let Israel be glad.* PSALM 14:7

God will restore your fortunes. Just keep focused on His faithfulness!

◇◇◇◇◇◇◇◇◇◇

*I will bring you health and will heal you of your wounds—
this is the LORD's declaration.* JEREMIAH 30:17

It is God's will that you be healed. Whether that healing
comes here or in heaven is up to Him.

◇◇◇◇◇◇◇◇◇◇

*"I will certainly bring health and healing to [the city]
and will indeed heal [God's people]. I will let them experience
the abundance of true peace.* JEREMIAH 33:6

True peace comes as we rest in the promises of God
and stay sensitive to His presence with us.
And praise Him! He has healed your soul!

Words of Life for Those
Needing Help

Fresh out of seminary, the young pastor pored over his notes. His teachers had taught him well and he relished the thought of planting a new church. But planning and planting a church in theory was far different from pulling it off in reality. How on earth was he going to get everything to fall into place as he envisioned? How was he going to get it off the ground?

Like all of us, he needs to remember where his help comes from. Whenever we're in a situation that's clearly over our heads, we instinctively turn to each other, to books, to tools, or whatever we can find to work out a way for us to win. But God's Spirit tells us to look in a different direction: up!

Throughout Scripture, we see how much God loves to help His people who ask Him for it. It's also full of stories of people who forgot God and tried to go it on their own. The differing results are dramatic. When we look to God for help in both the big and small events of our lives, we see heaven respond with supernatural strength and speed. God's help reaps eternal impact and strengthens our faith in the process.

I lift my eyes toward
the mountains.
Where will my
help come from?
My help comes
from the LORD,
the Maker of
heaven and earth.

Psalm 121:1-2

Life-Giving Words for Those *Needing Help*

He who calls you is faithful; He will do it. I Thessalonians 5:24

Whenever God calls you to do something, He will equip you
with everything you need to succeed.

<hr>

*Let us approach the throne of grace with boldness, so that we may receive mercy
and find grace to help us in time of need.* Hebrews 4:16

Don't be shy! Ask the Father for whatever you need because
He loves to give you the desires of your heart.

<hr>

*Those who trust in the Lord will renew their strength;
they will soar on wings like eagles; they will run and not become weary,
they will walk and not faint.* Isaiah 40:31

When you are weary, wait on God. Sit patiently in His presence.
Let His light flood the darkness. Let His presence
refresh you and fill you with hope.

<hr>

*My God will supply all your needs according to His riches
in glory in Christ Jesus.* Philippians 4:19

God never runs out of resources for you. After all,
the entire universe belongs to Him! Rely on Him.
Trust Him to supply whatever you need.

God is my Helper; the Lord is the Sustainer of my life. PSALM 54:4

Even when it looks like no one else is around, God is.
He is holding you, and He will bring you to a safe place.

◦◦◦◦◦◦◦◦◦◦◦

The Lord is my helper; I will not be afraid.
What can man do to me? HEBREWS 13:6

People may conspire against you, but God is for you—
and He always will be! You really have nothing to fear.

◦◦◦◦◦◦◦◦◦◦◦

Oh, Lord God! You yourself made the heavens and earth by Your great power and
with Your outstretched arm. Nothing is too difficult for You! JEREMIAH 32:17

What you're facing is too hard for you and me to figure out, but it's
not too hard for God. Let's ask Him for help right now!

◦◦◦◦◦◦◦◦◦◦◦

Cast your burden on the LORD, and He will sustain you; He will never allow
the righteous to be shaken. PSALM 55:22

We may not know what to do, but God will make a way
as we look to Him to help us and guide us.

◦◦◦◦◦◦◦◦◦◦◦

Unless the LORD builds a house, its builders labor over it in vain; unless the LORD
watches over a city, the watchman stays alert in vain. PSALM 127:1

We're wasting our efforts when we try to do life alone.
Let's ask God for help!

Words of Life for
Our Finances

They had thought about everything: venue, bridesmaid dresses, flowers, rings, DJ, photographer, videographer, reception, menu. They had so much to plan, but it was so much fun! Now that the wedding was over however, they realized one major oversight: they hadn't paid enough attention to the financial aspect of their big day. Immediately, their happily-ever-after was forced to deal with a bit of friction. As they talked over the best way to manage their money, they realized the significant differences in their attitudes toward money and the practices they'd grown up with.

Currently, one of the top reasons for divorces (Christian or not) is money. Our attitudes about money can impact the way we approach God, our spouse, our church, and our relationship with the world. God's Word says we need to be super careful about how we handle and think about money. In fact, the Bible contains more than 800 references to wealth! It can rule and ruin our lives, or it can fuel our efforts to reach the needy world around us with God's love and practical assistance.

Believers need each other to not only speak the truth about money management in love—we also need to live it out side by side. Let's start by reviewing some of God's main points about money management. Then we'll be better able to speak wise words of encouragement to ourselves as well as to others. It's important to our spiritual health that we buy into God's ways with money.

"Seek first the
kingdom of God and
His righteousness,
and all these things
will be provided
for you."

Matthew 6:33

Life-Giving Words for *Our Finances*

My God will supply all your needs according to His riches in glory in Christ Jesus. PHILIPPIANS 4:19

God knows what you truly need in this moment. Ask Him to provide for you and trust Him to supply what you lack.

∞∞∞∞∞

"Consider the birds of the sky: They don't sow or reap or gather into barns, yet your heavenly Father feeds them. Aren't you worth more than they?" MATTHEW 6:26

Look outside at this incredible world God has created— and He has sustained it from the beginning of time! Clearly, He is more than capable of managing our world of needs.

∞∞∞∞∞

Don't wear yourself out to get rich; because you know better, stop! As soon as your eyes fly to it, it disappears, for it makes wings for itself and flies like an eagle to the sky. PROVERBS 23:4-5

You have a tremendous work ethic, but you need a life too. Don't let worldly pursuits rob you of the joy God gives to those who make Him their first prioirity.

∞∞∞∞∞

"Bring the whole tithe into the storehouse, that there may be food in My house. Test Me in this," says the LORD Almighty, "and see if I will not throw open the floodgates of heaven and pour out so much blessing that there will not be room enough to store it." MALACHI 3:10 NIV

You have such a generous heart! Thank you for always sharing, always looking out for other people's needs, and always passing along what God has so generously given to you.

"No servant can serve two masters, since either he will hate one and love the other, or he will be devoted to one and despise the other. You cannot serve both God and money." LUKE 16:13

We see so clearly your love and commitment to God in the way you give.

✿✿✿✿✿✿✿

The love of money is a root of all kinds of evil, and by craving it, some have wandered away from the faith and pierced themselves with many griefs. I TIMOTHY 6:10

Watch out! The world tells us we need more money to be happy, but God knows better. We actually need more of Him!

✿✿✿✿✿✿✿

"Whoever is faithful in very little is also faithful in much, and whoever is unrighteous in very little is also unrighteous in much. So if you have not been faithful with worldly wealth, who will trust you with what is genuine?" LUKE 16:10-11

You are such a faithful steward of the resources God has given this family. Thank you for your example.

✿✿✿✿✿✿✿

Remember that the LORD your God gives you the power to gain wealth. DEUTERONOMY 8:18

Even though you're very gifted at what you do, I've noticed that you always give God the credit for your success. I'm sure He's pleased to see you using your talents for His kingdom and giving Him the glory.

Words of Life for the
Caregiver

At first, it was hardly noticeable and pretty normal. He'd forget where he left his keys or his wallet. But over time the situation grew worse: he'd forget where he parked his car, where he was, or why he had gone there in the first place. His concerned wife called the doctor, they ran some tests, and their worst fears were confirmed: early-onset Alzheimer's. Both of them knew that life would never be the same. He worried what kind of burden he'd become; she wondered how she'd manage.

Hopefully, they won't do it alone….

The caretaker's road is often long and lonely. Whether we're caring for someone with special needs, a mentally ill teen, an aging spouse, or even perfectly healthy but active children, continuously taking care of others drains us physically, emotionally, and spiritually. The workload often isolates us, and outsiders can't imagine the struggles happening in our home. No wonder we're easy prey for the enemy's arrows of discouragement or despair.

So let's consider people we know who are laboring daily to love others who can't do much, if anything, on their own. Ask the Lord to give these caregivers His strength, His love, and the ability to persevere. Let's also come alongside these people who are giving of themselves sacrificially. May we share God's grace, offer words of life to lift their spirits, pray for them, and maybe even relieve them of their duties for an hour or so.

LORD,
you understand;
remember me
and care for me.

Jeremiah 15:15 NIV

Life-Giving Words
for the *Caregiver*

"The King will answer [the righteous], 'Truly I tell you, whatever you did for one of the least of these brothers and sisters of mine, you did for me.'" MATTHEW 25:40

Jesus is a blessed Recipient of every kindness you extend. Serving "one of the least" is like serving Him.

∞∞∞∞∞∞∞

"This is my command: Love one another as I have loved you. No one has greater love than this: to lay down his life for his friends." JOHN 15:12-13

Your daily commitment to help the hurting and serve the needy helps me see Jesus better.

∞∞∞∞∞∞∞

I consider that the sufferings of this present time are not worth comparing with the glory that is going to be revealed to us. ROMANS 8:18

You're in a dark season right know. But joy lies on the other side of suffering. Keep seeking the Savior who has promised to reward those who don't lose hope!

∞∞∞∞∞∞∞

Trust in the LORD and do what is good; dwell in the land and live securely. PSALM 37:3

Don't be afraid of what's to come. God is your security, and all His plans for you are good.

The Lamb at the center of the throne will be their shepherd;
'He will lead them to springs of living water.' And God will wipe away
every tear from their eyes.'" REVELATION 7:17 NIV

A day is coming when all our tears will be wiped away.
Until then, I'm asking the Father to fill you with living streams
of His comfort and peace, His hope and strength.

∞∞∞∞∞∞∞

The LORD is my strength and my shield; my heart trusts in Him,
and I am helped. Therefore my heart celebrates,
and I give thanks to Him with my song. PSALM 28:7

Today is a gift from God to you. Celebrate the little signs
of His presence with you and love for you.

∞∞∞∞∞∞∞

Again Jesus said, "Simon son of John, do you love Me?"
He answered, "Yes, Lord, You know that I love You."
Jesus said, "Take care of My sheep." JOHN 21:16 NIV

You are a shepherd of one of God's precious sheep.
You bless our Savior with every tender touch and gentle word.

∞∞∞∞∞∞∞

Blessed is the one who endures trials, because when he has stood
the test he will receive the crown of life that God has promised
to those who love Him. JAMES 1:12

Hold on to hope! Jesus walks with you now and will
see you through this valley, providing His strength
and encouragement with each step.

Words of Life for
Our Leaders

Every Sunday he stands behind the pulpit, a smile on his face, God's Words of truth on his lips. His congregation truly appreciates him, patting him on the back or shaking his hand as they exit the sanctuary. But after they get in their car to go home, they rarely give their pastor a second thought.

One reason may be that our leaders at church, in government, at the office, and in the community seem larger than life—more like big-screen personalities playing a role than real human beings. But our pastors and teachers, police and military, bosses and politicians, even the President all bleed the same way we do and experience life's challenges, disappointments, joys, and sorrows like we all do.

These people are soldiers doing battle as they lead and protect the rest of us. They need our regular prayers as well as our encouragement and commendation—and not just at the end of a sermon or overseas tour of duty. They need our appreciation and support while they're still slugging it out in the trenches of life and the spotlight isn't shining on them. In those in-between moments, a word of encouragement can make a difference.

Remember your leaders who have spoken God's word to you. As you carefully observe the outcome of their lives, imitate their faith.

Hebrews 13:7

Life-Giving Words for *Our Leaders*

*How can they preach unless they are sent? As it is written:
How beautiful are the feet of those who bring good news.* ROMANS 10:15

People's lives are changed because you faithfully study
God's Word and share His truth with us.

<hr>

*If any of you lacks wisdom, he should ask God—who gives to all generously
and ungrudgingly—and it will be given to him.* JAMES 1:5

God will give you the wisdom you need to lead your family well,
even as you battle in your leadership role.

<hr>

He must increase, but I must decrease. JOHN 3:30

Your words and so many aspects of your life point me to Jesus.

<hr>

*"Whoever wants to become great among you
must be your servant."* MATTHEW 20:26

What I love most about your leadership style is your humility.
You value and respect people just as Jesus did.

<hr>

*Do nothing out of selfish ambition or conceit, but in humility consider others as
more important than yourselves. Everyone should look out not only for his own
interests, but also for the interests of others.* PHILIPPIANS 2:3-4

I appreciate the way you addressed our concerns
even though it didn't benefit you at all.

*Don't let anyone despise your youth, but set an example for the believers in speech,
in conduct, in love, in faith, and in purity.* I TIMOTHY 4:12

I see God raising you up to be a mighty leader for this lost generation.
Rely on Him to guide and empower!

⬥⬥⬥⬥⬥⬥⬥⬥

*Be diligent to present yourself to God as one approved, a worker who doesn't need
to be ashamed, correctly teaching the word of truth.* II TIMOTHY 2:15

I love that your walk is consistent with your talk.
Your messages are more powerful because of the ways
you love others throughout the week.

⬥⬥⬥⬥⬥⬥⬥⬥

*Know well the condition of your flock,
and pay attention to your herds.* PROVERBS 27:23

Thank you for taking time to listen to me.
I appreciate the way you care for the team!

⬥⬥⬥⬥⬥⬥⬥⬥

*"Even the Son of Man did not come to be served, but to serve,
and to give His life as a ransom for many."* MARK 10:45

Thank you for giving up your time and energy to serve us.

⬥⬥⬥⬥⬥⬥⬥⬥

*"So if I, your Lord and Teacher, have washed your feet,
you also ought to wash one another's feet."* JOHN 13:14

I'll do whatever you need me to do.
I want to support you any way I can.

Words of Life for the
Betrayed

How did I not see it coming? Sure, he'd been coming home *later and later each night. And there were those awkward gaps in his story when he'd explain where he'd been. But a full-blown affair? With her best friend?* The reality turned her whole world upside down, and her heart—as well as her hope for the future—shattered into a million pieces.

Perhaps nothing wounds our hearts more than betrayal, more than having someone we trusted prove to be unworthy of that trust. We thought we knew this person who turned on us so well. We find ourselves wondering who, if anyone, can actually be trusted.

Scripture tells us that we have a Friend who sticks closer than a brother, and this Friend knows firsthand the pain of a close friend's betrayal. So, in our pain and humiliation, He sits with us, comforting us through tender words of compassion, comforting our aching soul with His never-failing love.

And having received Jesus' comfort, we are to comfort others. We are privileged to represent Him as we hug, listen to, cry with, pray for, and speak beautiful truths that the betrayed need to hear: God sees and cares, He understands, and He mends those hearts that have been shattered into a million pieces.

One with many
friends may
be harmed,
but there is a friend
who stays closer
than a brother.

Proverbs 18:24

Life-Giving Words for the *Betrayed*

In return for my love, they accuse me, but I pray for them. PSALM 109:4 NOG

The intense pain of being betrayed is often beyond description.
Know that I'm asking Jesus to bless you with
His healing love and comforting peace. .

◇◇◇◇◇◇◇◇◇◇◇◇

*A false witness will not go unpunished, and one who
utters lies will not escape.* PROVERBS 19:5

God sees those who hurt you. May you rest knowing
that He will hold them accountable.

◇◇◇◇◇◇◇◇◇◇◇◇

*The Lord [God] was pleased to crush [Jesus] severely. When you make Him
a guilt offering, He will see His seed, He will prolong His days,
and by His hand, the Lord's pleasure will be accomplished.* ISAIAH 53:10

The Father used the Pharisees' evil to accomplish His plan to redeem
humankind. So I'm going to believe that your God and Defender
will one day turn the evil you've experienced into a blessing you can't
even imagine right now.

◇◇◇◇◇◇◇◇◇◇◇◇

*"Whenever you stand praying, if you have anything against anyone,
forgive him, so that your Father in heaven will also
forgive you your wrongdoing."* MARK 11:25

Grudges hold us prisoner, but forgiveness sets us free.

142

It is not an enemy who insults me—otherwise I could bear it; it is not a foe who rises up against me—otherwise I could hide from him. But it is you, a man who is my peer, my companion and good friend! We used to have close fellowship; we walked with the crowd into the house of God. PSALM 55:12-14

Lord, the person closest to me turned against me.
My heart is breaking and I feel like I can never trust
anyone again. Please come to my rescue!

✧✧✧✧✧✧✧✧✧

[Jesus] was troubled in His spirit and testified, "Truly I tell you, one of you will betray Me." JOHN 13:21

Jesus knows personally the deep pain of betrayal. His comfort
penetrates those unseen places where we hurt from being betrayed,
and His power and love enable us to heal.

✧✧✧✧✧✧✧✧✧

"You will be hated by all nations because of My name. Then many will fall away, betray one another, and hate one another. Many false prophets will rise up and deceive many. Because lawlessness will multiply, the love of many will grow cold. But the one who endures to the end will be saved." MATTHEW 24:9-13

Though the betrayal was intensely personal, the betrayer was also
turning on God—and God will hold him/her responsible for that
choice. God, whom you so faithfully serve, will bless you for your
faithfulness to Him even in this dark and painful season.

✧✧✧✧✧✧✧✧✧

You prepare a table before me in the presence of my enemies. PSALM 23:5

Though many you love forsake you, cling to the truth that
you have a constant friend in Jesus—and in me!
Jesus invites you to feast on His goodness while
your accusers watch in wonder.

Words of Life for the
Bitter

Her life had not been easy. Abuse and neglect seemed to have followed her since she first experienced them as a child. Now an adult, she found her heart too hardened by pain to open up to hope. She felt destined to lose at relationships and at life. Her face clearly revealed the bitter state of her soul, telling others not to dare to approach her.

Bitterness binds us in a vise-like grip of despair. But we don't have to stay there because God's love can break through! His powerful presence breaks the bonds of bitterness and His truth sets free those being held captive.

Whenever we find seeds of bitterness being sown in our heart or in someone else's, we can't stand idly, hoping they don't sprout, take root, and take over. Instead, we must search for the ungodly beliefs from which bitterness springs: *What am I honestly believing about God in this situation? Am I doubting His goodness, His forgiveness, or His love? Am I caught in the trap of unforgiveness?* As we speak the truth about God, our identity in Him, and the future He has promised, His Spirit can melt our barren winter of bitterness into a beautiful, life-giving springtime of hope.

It was for my own
well-being that I had such
intense bitterness;
but Your love has
delivered me from
the Pit of destruction,
for You have thrown all
my sins behind Your back.

Isaiah 38:17

Life-Giving Words for the *Bitter*

Let all bitterness, anger and wrath, shouting and slander be removed from you, along with all malice. And be kind and compassionate to one another, forgiving one another, just as God also forgave you in Christ. EPHESIANS 4:31-32

Bitterness reveals our distrust of God's goodness and His ability to redeem the years of the locusts. Remember, God is for you—and I'll believe that for you if you can't. I encourage you to ask Him to help you let go of the hurt and teach you to cling to Him instead.

<hr>

As God's chosen ones, holy and dearly loved, put on compassion, kindness, humility, gentleness, and patience, bearing with one another and forgiving one another if anyone has a grievance against another. Just as the Lord has forgiven you, so you are also to forgive. COLOSSIANS 3:12-13

God can help you choose compassion and forgiveness over bitterness. With this step toward freedom, you'll taste peace and joy.

<hr>

Husbands, love your wives and don't be bitter toward them. COLOSSIANS 3:19

I admire the way you always speak well of your spouse.

<hr>

But if you have bitter envy and selfish ambition in your heart, don't boast and deny the truth. JAMES 3:14

Thank you for being an example of how to live wisely in humility, participating in good works, enjoying peace, and giving the glory to God.

Abner called out to Joab: "Must the sword devour forever?
Don't you realize this will only end in bitterness? How long before you tell
the troops to stop pursuing their brothers?" "As God lives," Joab replied,
"if you had not spoken up, the troops wouldn't have stopped pursuing
their brothers until morning." II SAMUEL 2:26-27

I'm so glad you cared enough about our relationship to confront
the situation. Your courageous and wise move has kept
bitterness from taking root in both of us.

∞∞∞∞∞∞∞∞

The LORD saw that the affliction of Israel was very bitter for both slaves
and free people. There was no one to help Israel. II KINGS 14:26

God sees all your pain and suffering, and His heart is grieved.
Guard against bitterness toward Him. Choose instead to,
baby step by baby step, trust Him for your future.

∞∞∞∞∞∞∞∞

"Go and tell Hezekiah, 'This is what the LORD God of your
ancestor David says: I have heard your prayer; I have seen your tears.
Look, I am going to add fifteen years to your life.'" ISAIAH 38:5

God hears us when we pray, so let's go to Him together
and ask Him to help us forgive the people who hurt us.

∞∞∞∞∞∞∞∞

Pursue peace with everyone, and holiness—without it no one will see the Lord.
Make sure that no one falls short of the grace of God and that no root of
bitterness springs up, causing trouble and defiling many. HEBREWS 12:14-15

I am starting to feel bitter about this situation. Can we talk
about what happened and maybe even pray together?

Words of Life for
Friends

From the sound of her voice, her friend knew right away that something was wrong. Without being asked, she immediately went over. They knew each other so well, they hardly needed words. One talked, the other listened, and both cried as they shouldered this burden together. What a sacred, safe place God had given them in each other!

So it is in a strong friendship, the kind of heart connection that enables us to pick back up wherever you last left off, as if no time had passed. All friends are gifts from God. Some friends are gifts for a season, but our closest companions are life-giving blessings as they help us experience the depth and beauty of God's love.

Of course, forging such friendships takes time, persistence, and intentional interactions. But when God is involved in the foundation laying and construction project, your bond of friendship will never be broken—not for all eternity! Take time today to thank God for your friends and then share with them a truth from God's Word that will strengthen and encourage them.

Two are better than one
because they have a good
reward for their efforts.
For if either falls,
his companion can
lift him up; but pity
the one who falls without
another to lift him up.

Ecclesiastes 4:9-10

Life-Giving Words for *Friends*

I am a friend to all who fear you,
to those who keep your precepts. PSALM 119:63

Father, thank You for the fellowship
I always find with those who also love You.

∞∞∞∞∞∞∞∞

The one who walks with the wise will become wise,
but a companion of fools will suffer harm. PROVERBS 13:20

I always trust your advice because instead of following your own
thoughts and opinions, you rely on God's Word for direction.

∞∞∞∞∞∞∞∞

One with many friends may be harmed,
but there is a friend who stays closer than a brother. PROVERBS 18:24

Thank you for always being there for me.
If it weren't for you and the Lord, I don't know what I'd do.

∞∞∞∞∞∞∞∞

The wounds of a friend are trustworthy,
but the kisses of an enemy are excessive. PROVERBS 27:6

What you're saying hurts, but I trust your heart. So I'm going
to pray about whether or not the Lord agrees with your perspective.
I may soon be thanking you for pointing out a blind spot in my life!

∞∞∞∞∞∞∞∞

Oil and incense bring joy to the heart, and the sweetness of a friend
is better than self-counsel. PROVERBS 27:9

I feel so much better now that I've talked to you about it.

No one is to seek his own good, but the good
of the other person. I Corinthians 10:24

The way you always put the needs of others first truly amazes
and inspires me. I see Jesus in your servant's heart!

∞∞∞∞∞∞∞

How good and pleasant it is
when brothers live together in harmony! Psalm 133:1

I love how you seem to know what I'm thinking
without me even saying a word.

∞∞∞∞∞∞∞

A friend loves at all times,
and a brother is born for a difficult time. Proverbs 17:17

When everyone else left me, you stayed.
You are a rare and true friend. I thank God for you.

∞∞∞∞∞∞∞

Carry one another's burdens; in this way you will
fulfill the law of Christ. Galatians 6:2

I can tell something's weighing you down. You can trust me.
Tell me what's troubling you and let me share the load.

∞∞∞∞∞∞∞

Iron sharpens iron, and one person sharpens another. Proverbs 27:17

You help me see and consider things about my
shortcomings and weaknesses that I never would notice
on my own. Thank you!

Words of Life for Those
Who Doubt

During Bible study, he seemed strangely quiet. While everyone else chattered away about the week's events, he seemed lost in his own world. At one point, the leader pulled him aside to ask if something was bothering him. Something was—but he struggled to identify it.

"I'm just having trouble...with my faith, I guess," he finally said. "No matter how much I pray, God never seems to answer. And I don't see, much less experience, all the victory everyone around me talks about. I'm stuck in the same sins I've struggled with all my life. And I can't stop thinking, *What if the whole God thing isn't real?*"

If we're honest with ourselves, we all have had times of doubt. Believing in something we can't fully prove and trusting Someone we can't see isn't always easy, especially when life seems out of control. But that's exactly why we need each other. When a friend is struggling to believe, we can help them remember ways God has proven Himself all throughout history as well as in their lives. Also, sharing truths from His Word, coupled with an encouraging hug, helps strengthen our own faith as well as that of the friend who is struggling with doubts.

We walk by faith, not by sight.

II Corinthians 5:7

Life-Giving Words for Those *Who Doubt*

[God's] invisible attributes, that is, His eternal power and divine nature, have been clearly seen since the creation of the world, being understood through what He has made. As a result, people are without excuse. ROMANS 1:20

Consider the intricacy, beauty, and order of the world you see outside.
Think about the complexity of the eyeball or the atom.
Let the visual splendor and the mind-boggling detail of creation
inform your mind and heart of their magnificent Designer.

∞∞∞∞∞∞∞∞

Now the serpent was the most cunning of all the wild animals that the Lord God had made. He said to the woman, "Did God really say, 'You can't eat from any tree in the garden'?" GENESIS 3:1

Satan always tries to get us to question God's goodness.
Don't listen to the Deceiver. Our unchanging God has
always been and will always be good.

∞∞∞∞∞∞∞∞

"My people have committed a double evil: They have abandoned Me, the fountain of living water, and dug cisterns for themselves— cracked cisterns that cannot hold water. JEREMIAH 2:13

Have you found any better alternative than Jesus,
anything that satisfies your soul more than the Lord does?

∞∞∞∞∞∞∞∞

*I rise before dawn and cry out for help;
I put my hope in Your word.* PSALM 119:147

Don't be afraid to tell God your doubts. He won't love you any less.
(That's impossible!) And ask Him to increase your faith as you study
His Word. He will surely and gladly help you.

Woe to those who go down to Egypt for help and who depend on horses! They trust in the abundance of chariots and in the large number of horsemen. They do not look to the Holy One of Israel and they do not seek the LORD. ISAIAH 31:1

It's tempting to look at statistics, to consider circumstances, and then conclude that we need to take matters into our own hands. But God wants us to look to Him instead. Our help comes from Him alone.

∞∞∞∞∞∞∞∞

Be aware of this: Scoffers will come in the last days scoffing and following their own evil desires, saying, "Where is His 'coming' that He promised? Ever since our ancestors fell asleep, all things continue as they have been since the beginning of creation." II Peter 3:3-4

God warns us that, in the end days, many people will become cynical about whether He will fulfill His promises. Of course He will— and He delights in His people who hold firmly to truth.

∞∞∞∞∞∞∞∞

We also have the prophetic word strongly confirmed, and you will do well to pay attention to it, as to a lamp shining in a dark place, until the day dawns and the morning star rises in your hearts. II PETER 1:19

Did you know that Jesus Christ fulfilled more than 350 Old Testament prophecies? What are the odds!

∞∞∞∞∞∞∞∞

Immediately Jesus reached out His hand, caught hold of [Peter], and said to him, "You of little faith, why did you doubt?" When they got into the boat, the wind ceased. Then those in the boat worshiped Him and said, "Truly You are the Son of God." MATTHEW 14:31-33

Remember the ways God has shown you His faithfulness. Recount examples from your life as well as examples from history.

Words of Life for the
Devastated

When Martha and Mary sent word to Jesus that Lazarus was deathly ill, Jesus *waited*. By the time He finally arrived to His friends' home, Lazarus had been dead for four days. Hundreds of mourners wailed, but the worst moment for Jesus may have been when He saw His two beloved friends, Mary and Martha, so devastated by their brother's death. Touched to the core, Jesus wept along with them even though He knew the good that was about to happen.

As Jesus clearly revealed in this interaction with Mary and Martha, God cares about our hurts, and He understands how deeply the tragedies in life affect us. So He comes, walks with us, and weeps with us. In His humanity, Jesus relates to our pain, and in His divinity, He redeems life's pain to reveal God's glory. Just as Jesus spoke and raised Lazarus from the grave, His words continue to bring light and life even when we're living through our darkest nightmares.

Let's remember that when our friends experience tragedy, we are treading on sacred ground. We don't need to solve any problem. What is most helpful is to simply sit with them just as our Savior sits with us. Sharing their pain in that way is an act of love and empathy speaks volumes. Then, if the Spirit leads, we might whisper words of hope and life to lift their eyes to the Savior who sees them, loves them, and will heal their broken hearts.

Though he
slay me,
I will hope
in him.

Job 13:15 ESV

Life-Giving Words for the *Devastated*

LORD God of Armies, who is strong like You, LORD? Your faithfulness surrounds You. You rule the raging sea; when its waves surge, You still them. PSALM 89:8-9

God is still on the throne. Listen for the King's voice: He will speak peace to the storm raging in your soul right now.

✦✦✦✦✦✦✦✦✦

I am persuaded that neither death nor life, nor angels nor rulers, nor things present nor things to come, nor powers, nor height nor depth, nor any other created thing will be able to separate us from the love of God that is in Christ Jesus our Lord. ROMANS 8:38-39

Nothing in Heaven, on earth, or under the earth can keep God from loving you. You are His chosen, His beloved, His child… forever.

✦✦✦✦✦✦✦✦✦

Blessed be the God and Father of our Lord Jesus Christ. Because of His great mercy He has given us new birth into a living hope through the resurrection of Jesus Christ from the dead. I PETER 1:3

We have living hope because Jesus lives, Conqueror of sin and death, and He is with the Father, interceding for you right now!

✦✦✦✦✦✦✦✦✦

Whatever was written in the past was written for our instruction, so that we may have hope through endurance and through the encouragement from the Scriptures. ROMANS 15:4

When we endure tough times with hope, we have an opportunity to see God reveal Himself in miraculous ways, just as we see in the Scriptures.

*May our Lord Jesus Christ Himself and God our Father, who has loved us
and given us eternal encouragement and good hope by grace, encourage your hearts
and strengthen you in every good work and word.* II Thessalonians 2:16-17

I'm asking God the Father, God the Son, and God the Holy Spirit
to surround you with comfort, encourage your soul,
and strengthen you for the days ahead.

⬦⬦⬦⬦⬦⬦⬦⬦⬦

*Let us be self-controlled and put on the armor of faith and love,
and a helmet of the hope of salvation.* I Thessalonians 5:8

Put on your armor! We can defeat despair using our
three greatest weapons: faith, hope, and love.

⬦⬦⬦⬦⬦⬦⬦⬦⬦

*We do not want you to be uninformed, brothers and sisters,
concerning those who are asleep, so that you will not grieve like the rest,
who have no hope.* I Thessalonians 4:13

Even in the aching sadness that comes with a loved one's death,
we do not drown in despair. A day is coming when
we will see each other again, this time in glory.

⬦⬦⬦⬦⬦⬦⬦⬦⬦

*The Lord will send His faithful love by day; His song will be with me
in the night— a prayer to the God of my life.* Psalm 42:8

All day and throughout the night, the Lord watches over you and
sings His songs of love to soothe your soul. Listen for the music.

⬦⬦⬦⬦⬦⬦⬦⬦⬦

*I called to the Lord in my distress, and I cried to my
God for help. From His temple He heard my voice,
and my cry to Him reached His ears.* Psalm 18:6

Pour out your heart to the Lord because
He hears, He cares, and He will be near you.

159

Words of Life to
Bring Joy

Everyone circled around the boardroom table. The mood was tense and the meeting's agenda revealed all that was at stake. As she readied herself for her part of the presentation, she felt her stomach churn.

At that very second, her phone flashed and her eyes caught the screen. She saw a snapshot of her best friend's "silly face," the one that always made her laugh. This friend's thoughtful gesture worked; the timing had been perfect! Something about that connection with her friend relieved her of some stress, and she faced the room with confidence. Whatever happened in the meeting, she knew that she was loved.

Sometimes when we face the life's mountainous challenges, our perspective makes all the difference. Even in the middle of the most trying circumstances, God longs for us to feel the joy of His presence. His loyalty, power, and unrelenting love can bless our soul with joy, no matter what is happening around us.

Let's be honest. Everywhere we turn and from all directions, we hear news that makes us never want to leave our house. But when we stress and worry, we are forgetting the Source of our strength: God's joy! Let's constantly remind ourselves—and our loved ones—how much fun it is to live and laugh in the Lord!

Now may the God
of hope fill you with
all joy and peace
as you believe so that
you may overflow
with hope by the power
of the Holy Spirit.

Romans 15:13

Life-Giving Words to *Bring Joy*

When I am filled with cares, Your comfort brings me joy. PSALM 94:19

I feel so much better knowing you care about me and will support me no matter what. You are a breath of fresh air to my soul!

oooooooooooooo

I have no greater joy than this: to hear that my children are walking in truth. III JOHN 1:4

I love to see you seeking Jesus with all your heart and standing firm in your faith just like you're doing. The way you live out your faith brings me unspeakable joy!

oooooooooooooo

Now to Him who is able to protect you from stumbling and to make you stand n the presence of His glory, without blemish and with great joy, to the only God our Savior, through Jesus Christ our Lord, be glory, majesty, power, and authority before all time, now and forever. Amen. JUDE 1:24-25

Whatever the headlines and despite the doom that is forecasted on talk radio, we don't need to be discouraged. God is going to finish what He has started in each of us, the good work of making us more like Jesus. We also know that one day all of His kids will stand before Him spotless and ready to rejoice for all eternity!

oooooooooooooo

Though I have many things to write to you, I don't want to use paper and ink. Instead, I hope to come to you and talk face to face so that our joy may be complete. II JOHN 1:12

Texting is great, but I most love spending time with you in person. When can we get together?

Consider it a great joy, my brothers and sisters, whenever you
experience various trials, because you know that the testing
of your faith produces endurance. JAMES 1:2-3

Let this trial prompt you to look upward to your heavenly Father.
Clearly, He has found you fit for training you up in
His kingdom ways. This difficult season challenges your
trust in His infinite love. He is growing your faith.

∞∞∞∞∞∞∞

Though you have not seen [the resurrected Jesus], you love Him;
though not seeing Him now, you believe in Him, and you rejoice
with inexpressible and glorious joy,   because you are receiving the goal
of your faith, the salvation of your souls. I PETER 1:8-9

Think about a time you felt so much joy you could hardly speak.
Heaven will be like that… times infinity.

∞∞∞∞∞∞∞

"There will be more joy in heaven over one sinner who repents than over
ninety-nine righteous people who don't need repentance." LUKE 15:7

I am so thrilled that you've become a Christian! My heart is literally
soaring with hope and joy for all that has now become yours as a
child of God. Welcome to Jesus' forever famly!

∞∞∞∞∞∞∞

Then [Nehemiah] said to [the people], "Go and eat what is rich,
drink what is sweet, and send portions to those who have nothing prepared,
since today is holy to our Lord. Do not grieve, because the joy
of the LORD is your strength." NEHEMIAH 8:10

God, in the same way that this food gives strength
and delight to our physical bodies, the joy of
Your presence fuels our souls!

Words of Life That
Inspire Worship

As the music plays and the worship leaders sing, we
feel our spirits swell with hope. In ways beyond description,
we are profoundly aware of God's presence with us as we, His
people, together declare His praise. As promised, His presence
brings us peace and perspective that deepen our trust and turn
our eyes toward Him, the only One worthy of our adoration.

But worship experiences don't only happen during music sets
at church. We worship our Lord wherever we are, whatever
we're doing, when we acknowledge with wonder who He is
and the grace of His love. Sometimes at such a moment, we
find a kindred spirit—a God-worshipper who also marvels
at His beauty. It's a divine appointment to praise God
together. It's a taste eternity in the middle of a ordinary
day's usual routine.

By singing or speaking the truth about God's greatness, we
spread the fragrance of His beautiful presence everywhere
we go. May the words of our mouth flow forth in a steady
stream of uplifting worship, welcoming those around us to
join in the celebration.

Let everything
that breathes
praise the LORD.
Hallelujah!

Psalm 150:6

Life-Giving Words That *Inspire Worship*

Come, let us worship and bow down;
let us kneel before the LORD our Maker. PSALM 95:6

We love our church and think you'd love it too.
Are you available to come with us this Sunday?

∞∞∞∞∞∞∞∞∞

"God is spirit, and those who worship Him must worship
in Spirit and in truth." JOHN 4:24

The Holy Spirit helps us connect with our Father as we seek
to know His heart through Scripture and songs.

∞∞∞∞∞∞∞∞∞

My soul, bless the LORD, and all that is within me,
bless His holy name. PSALM 103:1

Every part of me wants to shout and clap for joy when
I think about how much Jesus has done for me. He has
set me free from sin and darkness and death!

∞∞∞∞∞∞∞∞∞

Be filled by the Spirit: speaking to one another in psalms, hymns,
and spiritual songs, singing and making music with your heart
to the Lord, giving thanks always for everything to God the Father
in the name of our Lord Jesus Christ, submitting to one another
in the fear of Christ. EPHESIANS 5:18-21

Your love for Jesus is not only evident in what you do. I also hear it
as you sing—and I love that you sing almost everywhere you go!

For from Him and through Him and to Him are all things.
To Him be the glory forever. Amen. ROMANS 11:36

Everything we eat, drink, say, think, and do is a form of worship.
Let's worship wholeheartedly and glorify our God!

∞∞∞∞∞∞∞

Yours, LORD, is the greatness and the power and the glory and the splendor and the
majesty, for everything in the heavens and on earth belongs to You. Yours, LORD,
is the kingdom, and You are exalted as head over all. I CHRONICLES 29:11

Sometimes when I worship, I picture Jesus and the Father, seated
on their heavenly thrones, as all of creation bows in reverence.

∞∞∞∞∞∞∞

You, God, are my God, earnestly I seek You; I thirst for You, my whole being longs
for You, in a dry and parched land where there is no water. PSALM 63:1 NIV

The deepest longings in my heart are only satisfied at God's throne
as I worship in awe and wonder and gratitude.

∞∞∞∞∞∞∞

Present your bodies as a living sacrifice, holy and pleasing to God;
this is your true worship. Do not be conformed to this age, but be transformed
by the renewing of your mind, so that you may discern what is the good,
pleasing, and perfect will of God. ROMANS 12:1-2

I love that you not only study God's Word,
but live it out in all areas of your life.

∞∞∞∞∞∞∞

Let the whole earth shout triumphantly to the LORD! Serve the LORD
with gladness; come before Him with joyful songs. PSALM 100:1-2

I would be happy to help you! It's my joy and privilege to
serve my God by serving my brothers and sisters in Christ.

Words of Life That
Release Forgiveness

As he looked around the room at all his brothers,
Joseph realized he had waited for this moment his entire life.
Though all were much older now, Joseph still recognized
each one and remembered all too well the day they sold him
as a slave to some foreigners passing by. After years in slavery
and in prison, Joseph now stood before them as the ruler
over them.

If anyone had a reason to hold a grudge or exact retribution
for a wrong done to him, it was Joseph. The course of his
entire life took an abrupt turn the day his brothers betrayed
him. But Joseph didn't grow bitter because despite their cruel
act, he looked for and saw his good God's sovereign hand
guiding his steps. By choosing to trust his heavenly Father,
Joseph was freed to forgive his offenders.

Jesus has much to say about forgiveness, but His own life
speaks the loudest as He forgave the people who persecuted
Him even as He hung on the cross. In doing so, Jesus showed
us the glory of God revealed when we forgive our offenders
and release them into His care. When we face those who've
hurt us, we can choose to forgive, and that's a choice to let
God's love and forgiveness flow through us.

"Come, let us settle this,"
says the LORD.
"Though your sins
are scarlet, they will
be as white as snow;
though they are
crimson red,
they will be like wool."

Isaiah 1:18

Life-Giving Words That *Release Forgiveness*

*As God's chosen ones, holy and dearly loved, put on compassion, kindness,
humility, gentleness, and patience, bearing with one another and forgiving
one another if anyone has a grievance against another. Just as the Lord
has forgiven you, so you are also to forgive.* COLOSSIANS 3:12-13

Hey, it's okay. All's forgiven. I'm actually glad to have this opportunity
to share the grace God has poured out on me with you!

⬥⬥⬥⬥⬥⬥⬥

*"Be on your guard. If your brother sins, rebuke him, and if he repents, forgive him.
And if he sins against you seven times in a day, and comes back to you seven times,
saying, 'I repent,' you must forgive him."* LUKE 17:3-4

I do forgive you. And I really appreciate that you're
willing to apologize. We all make mistakes.

⬥⬥⬥⬥⬥⬥⬥

*"If you forgive others their offenses, your heavenly Father will
forgive you as well. But if you don't forgive others, your Father
will not forgive your offenses."* MATTHEW 6:14-15

Whenever you're tempted to hold onto a grudge,
remember how many of your sins God has forgiven
and released. We experience a fuller relationship
with the Father when we choose to forgive.

⬥⬥⬥⬥⬥⬥⬥

*"I, even I, am He who blots out your transgressions, for My own sake,
and remembers your sins no more."* ISAIAH 43:25 NIV

God forgives us simply because He wants to. The darker our sin,
the brighter His grace shines.

If we confess our sins, He is faithful and righteous to forgive us
our sins and to cleanse us from all unrighteousness. I JOHN 1:9

Don't let Satan lie to you. You have been completely forgiven; you
have no reason to feel shame. In fact, God nailed
your guilt and shame—and mine—to the cross
so that we stand before Him blameless and pure.

∞∞∞∞∞∞∞∞

Let all bitterness, anger and wrath, shouting and slander be removed from you,
along with all malice. And be kind and compassionate to one another, forgiving one
another, just as God also forgave you in Christ. EPHESIANS 4:31-32

Even though it would be so easy to retaliate, leave that
judgment to God. Instead, for the sake of unity among
God's people, extend kindness and compassion.

∞∞∞∞∞∞∞∞

Repent and turn back, so that your sins may be wiped out, that seasons
of refreshing may come from the presence of the Lord. ACTS 3:19-20

When you feel restless in your soul, ask God to search your heart
and show you anything that might be blocking the flow
of His love to you and through you.

∞∞∞∞∞∞∞∞

In Him we have redemption through His blood, the forgiveness of our trespasses,
according to the riches of His grace that He richly poured out on us with all
wisdom and understanding. EPHESIANS 1:7-8

Jesus knows exactly what we need for inner healing,
for complete healing. When we honestly face
our hurts and humbly yield ourselves before Him,
He makes us whole again.

Words of Life for the
Generous

The missionary from Uganda stood in front of her class, showing the students pictures and telling them stories about his work in Africa. Living in extremely impoverished conditions, many people from his village had little food and no shoes at all. As the young girl listened intently, tears filled her eyes and resolve filled her heart. When she got home, she searched between the sofa cushions, emptied her piggy bank, and asked her parents to donate the money they normally spent on her birthday to the missionary's cause.

Such selflessness seems less apparent in our affluent culture. We strategize how to keep our treasure, time, and talents to ourselves and our family. We serve an incredibly generous God, who longs to see His heart reflected as His people give to others in need, yet we readily hold back.

Jesus, however, saw God's generous heart when He watched the widow put her two mites into the temple treasury. She didn't hold back; she trusted God to meet her needs. And Jesus commended her to His disciples.

We are to follow the example of the widow and the young girl. May we also notice both the big ways and the small ways the people around us give generously of their treasure, time, and talents. And when we notice, let's both encourage them to continue giving and join them in the joy of giving for the good of those we help and for God's glory.

A generous person
will be enriched,
and the one who
gives a drink of water
will receive water.

Proverbs 11:25

Life-Giving Words for the *Generous*

Each person should do as he has decided in his heart—not reluctantly or out of compulsion, since God loves a cheerful giver. II CORINTHIANS 9:7

I appreciate that you open the door for others and greet them with a smile each day. Your joy is contagious!

<hr/>

"Give, and it will be given to you; a good measure—pressed down, shaken together, and running over—will be poured into your lap. For with the measure you use, it will be measured back to you." LUKE 6:38

We read in Psalm 50 that God owns "the cattle on a thousand hills." That's a Hebrew way of saying that everything belongs to God, the Creator and Sustainer of the universe! So of course we can never outgive God! Furthermore, He loves to bless those who bless others.

<hr/>

"Whoever gives even a cup of cold water to one of these little ones because he is a disciple, truly I tell you, he will never lose his reward." MATTHEW 10:42

God sees the ways you care for His people and your faithfulness in praying for them. This kingdom work you're doing will reap great reward now and in the age to come.

<hr/>

Don't neglect to do what is good and to share, for God is pleased with such sacrifices. HEBREWS 13:16

Thank you so much for sharing your home with us. Your hospitality opens the door for many people to know God.

You will be enriched in every way for all generosity, which produces thanksgiving to God through us. II CORINTHIANS 9:11

May God prosper all the work of your hands so that with your surplus, you can bless many others.

∞∞∞∞∞∞∞∞∞

If the eagerness is there, the gift is acceptable according to what a person has, not according to what he does not have. II CORINTHIANS 8:12

We might not have much, but the same God who multiplied the fish and the loaves to feed thousands can take what we give and change the world.

∞∞∞∞∞∞∞∞∞

Kindness to the poor is a loan to the LORD, and He will give a reward to the lender. PROVERBS 19:17

God pays back our generosity with divine interest!

∞∞∞∞∞∞∞∞∞

"Bring the full tenth into the storehouse so that there may be food in my house. Test me in this way," says the LORD of Armies. "See if I will not open the floodgates of heaven and pour out a blessing for you without measure." MALACHI 3:10

Don't give what you don't have, but trust God to bless your generosity with what you do have. God is a lavish and faithful Rewarder!

∞∞∞∞∞∞∞∞∞

"Give to everyone who asks you, and from someone who takes your things, don't ask for them back." LUKE 6:30

"I'd be happy to give that to you. God bless you!"

Words of Life for the
Powerless/Weak

The wife watched as her husband and father of their three young children drove off into the night. As the wife of an active-duty military man, she knew the drill, but experience didn't make the separation any easier. Whenever he stepped forward into soldier duties, she stepped into single-mom mode, wondering where she'd find the strength to make it through another tour of duty. Or even through another day, for that matter.

Truth be told, none of us like feeling powerless. We work hard to make sure we've done what we can to make life easy for ourselves and our loved ones. But life throws us some crazy curveballs. And God, in His merciful sovereignty, uses them to show us a truth that we like to ignore, a truth that our souls need to know: we are weak. Needy. Downright desperate.

At the same time though, God's immeasurable strength, steady and certain, is always available to us through His Spirit. Discovering our weakness need not lead to despair. Instead, as Paul said, we can learn to delight in those very weaknesses. When we speak the truth of God's presence and power over our weaknesses, we watch a power greater than anything in this world work wonders in us and through us.

My flesh and
my heart may fail,
but God is the
Strength of
my heart and my
Portion forever.

Psalm 73:26 NIV

Life-Giving Words for the *Powerless/Weak*

*[The LORD] gives strength to the faint
and strengthens the powerless.* ISAIAH 40:29

You have been working and fighting for so long. No wonder
you're exhausted. Let's pray and ask God to renew your strength.

∞∞∞∞∞∞∞

*"Come to Me, all of you who are weary and burdened, and I will give you rest.
Take up My yoke and learn from Me, because I am lowly and humble in heart,
and you will find rest for your souls."* MATTHEW 11:28-29

Jesus invites us to enjoy a deep and lasting soul-rest.
But if we are to receive it, we need to relax our grip
on control of our lives and open our hand.

∞∞∞∞∞∞∞

*In the same way the Spirit also helps us in our weakness,
because we do not know what to pray for as we should, but the Spirit Himself
intercedes for us with unspoken groanings.* ROMANS 8:26

You don't have to have the right words when you pray.
God not only understands your heart, but through
His all-knowing Spirit, He also fills in the gap when your
words fall short. In other words, God Himself prays for you!

∞∞∞∞∞∞∞

*"Stay awake and pray, so that you won't enter into temptation.
The spirit is willing, but the flesh is weak."* MATTHEW 26:41

The powers of evil around us are too great for us to
go alone in this world. Let's pray together for
God's protection and the strength to persevere.

178

Do not fear, for I am with you; do not be afraid, for I am your God.
I will strengthen you; I will help you; I will hold on to you
with my righteous right hand. ISAIAH 41:10

Let you fears dissolve in the fact that God is for you, He is with you,
and He Himself will strengthen you for whatever the task at hand.

∞∞∞∞∞∞∞∞∞

[The Lord] said to me, "My grace is sufficient for you, for My power is
perfected in weakness." Therefore, I will most gladly boast all the more about
my weaknesses, so that Christ's power may reside in me. So I take pleasure in
weaknesses, insults, hardships, persecutions, and in difficulties, for the sake of
Christ. For when I am weak, then I am strong. II CORINTHIANS 12:9-10

Be glad that you're in over your head! That kind of experience
helps you recognize just how much you need Jesus and now
you'll get to watch Him work in a way that only He can.

∞∞∞∞∞∞∞∞∞

Youths may become faint and weary, and young men stumble and fall,
but those who trust in the LORD will renew their strength; they will soar
on wings like eagles; they will run and not become weary,
they will walk and not faint. ISAIAH 40:30-31

I'm praying for God to renew your strength in such a way
that you not only finish, but flourish in the process!

∞∞∞∞∞∞∞∞∞

No discipline seems pleasant at the time, but painful.
Later on, however, it produces a harvest of righteousness and peace
for those who have been trained by it. Therefore, strengthen your
feeble arms and weak knees. HEBREWS 12:11-12 NIV

Don't let this setback defeat you or define you. Our good
Father disciplines us because He has great plans for us.

Words of Life for When
Loved Ones Leave

From the day she first held her baby boy in her arms, she dreamed of the man he would become. Now, eighteen years later, she looked at boy-turned-young-man standing before her, and she smiled. Proudly wearing his cap and gown, he smiled broadly, eyes wide with excitement. He was ready to spread his wings and fly.

And now, as he was leaving to live on his own, what could she say? Of all the advice and instruction she'd offered through the years, what was most important for him to remember?

Solomon must have felt the same sense of urgency as he wrote out words of wisdom for his own sons who would one day be leaders in the kingdom. Consistent with countless other Scripture passages, Solomon's wisdom still speaks purpose, purity, and power into our lives today.

When our loved ones are poised to leave—whether for a short trip to school or for the great unknown—may our words share the wisdom of God and the reminder that He's with them wherever they go.

"May the LORD bless you
and protect you;
may the LORD make
His face shine on you
and be gracious to you;
may the LORD look
with favor on you
and give you peace."

Numbers 6:24-26

Life-Giving Words for When *Loved Ones Leave*

Now may the God of peace Himself sanctify you completely.
And may your whole spirit, soul, and body be kept sound and blameless
at the coming of our Lord Jesus Christ. I THESSALONIANS 5:23

Our Father will finish the transformational work He has begun
in you. As He continues to make you more like Jesus, we trust
Him to also guard you and guide you physically,
emotionally, and spiritually everywhere you go.

∞∞∞∞∞∞∞∞∞

May the Lord of peace Himself give you peace always in every way.
The Lord be with all of you. II THESSALONIANS 3:16

As you embark on this new adventure, may God's peace fill you
and may His grace keep you focused on His presence with you!

∞∞∞∞∞∞∞∞∞

There were many tears shed by everyone. They embraced Paul
and kissed him, grieving most of all over his statement
that they would never see his face again. ACTS 20:37-38

Though my heart aches as we close this chapter and start another,
I'm trusting the Lord to take even better care of you than I could.

∞∞∞∞∞∞∞∞∞

Be strengthened by the Lord and by His vast strength. Put on the full armor of
God so that you can stand against the schemes of the devil. EPHESIANS 6:10-11

Though you may feel alone at times, remember that God never leaves
you. He also equips you with His truth and the strength you need
to fight well against any evil you encounter on the road ahead.

"For I know the plans I have for you"—this is the LORD's declaration—
plans for your well-being, not for disaster,
to give you a future and a hope." JEREMIAH 29:11

The future may be unknown to us, but your heavenly Father's faithfulness is certain. He has good plans for you and His Spirit will guide you to them as you trust and listen for His direction.

∞∞∞∞∞∞∞

A person's steps are established by the LORD,
and he takes pleasure in His way. PSALM 37:23

Don't worry. You don't have to have everything in life all figured out. Besides, the Lord knows what's best for you. Just keep your eyes on Him and He will lead you where you need to go.

∞∞∞∞∞∞∞

The grace of the Lord Jesus be with everyone. Amen. REVELATION 22:21

God blesses His children with His grace. In fact,
if we could go anywhere in this entire universe,
we would never be separated from His love.

∞∞∞∞∞∞∞

Peace to the brothers and sisters, and love with faith, from God the Father
and the Lord Jesus Christ. Grace be with all who have undying love
for our Lord Jesus Christ. EPHESIANS 6:23-24

We aren't designed to live in isolation. Seek out
a Christian community in the city where God takes you.
Let God use your gifts to bless your fellow believers.

Words of Life for the
Spiritually Weary

He didn't want to admit it. After all, he was the leader
of their home, an elder in their church, and the one all his
buddies looked to for wisdom and advice whenever they
needed it. But lately, he had started to feel the weight of it all,
and he was tired of being the strong one, tired of trying to
keep everything together. He was worn out and weary....

God understands. One time when Moses grew weary trying
to manage the countless issues the new nation of Israel
encountered in the wilderness, God sent Jethro, Moses' father-
in-law, to speak words of wisdom and life he needed to hear:
*The work is too much for you, too much for any individual to bear on his
own.* Then Jethro taught this godly leader how to lean on God
as well as His people for the support he needed.

We can be that support for spiritually weary people when we
recognize their need. So ask the Lord to open your eyes to
those around you who work tirelessly for the kingdom. Then
take initiative to encourage them to keep going, not in their
own strength, but in the power of the One who sees them and
provides the support they need.

Let us not get
tired of doing good,
for we will reap
at the proper time
if we don't give up.

Galatians 6:9

Life-Giving
Words for the
Spiritually Weary

*Brother, may I benefit from you in the Lord;
refresh my heart in Christ.* PHILEMON 1:20

I want you to know that your patience and kindness encourages my heart and nourishes my soul. You make me want to know Jesus more!

∞∞∞∞∞∞∞

I am at rest in God alone; my salvation comes from Him. PSALM 62:1

Please take time in God's presence to rest and refresh yourself.
You need strength for the fight!

∞∞∞∞∞∞∞

*Do not lack diligence in zeal; be fervent in the Spirit;
serve the Lord.* ROMANS 12:11

You've been doing an amazing job here.
Keep up the good work!

∞∞∞∞∞∞∞

*Blessed be the LORD! He has given rest to His people Israel according
to all He has said. Not one of all the good promises He made through
His servant Moses has failed.* I KINGS 8:56

Let the promises of your faithful God reassure your heart and mind.
He will carry you through this.

∞∞∞∞∞∞∞

"I satisfy the thirsty person and feed all those who are weak." JEREMIAH 31:25

Come to the Lord's table and drink from His river of grace.
Let His love refresh your soul and strengthen your resolve.

Unless the LORD builds a house, its builders labor over it in vain;
unless the LORD watches over a city, the watchman stays alert in vain.
In vain you get up early and stay up late, working hard to have
enough food—yes, He gives sleep to the one He loves. PSALM 127:1-2

Trust the Lord to bless the work of your hands and leave your worries
at the foot of His throne. As you regularly remind us, He is faithful!

∞∞∞∞∞∞∞

Strengthen your tired hands and weakened knees,
and make straight paths for your feet, so that what is lame
may not be dislocated but healed instead. HEBREWS 12:12-13

Don't try to determine your course too far into the future.
Just take the next step as God's Spirit leads you and
as Jesus accompanies. In His presence is fullness of joy,
and that joy will give you strength.

∞∞∞∞∞∞∞

[The LORD] replied "My presence will go with you,
and I will give you rest." EXODUS 33:14

What a relief! No matter where we go, we always
find rest in the presence of God who goes with us.

∞∞∞∞∞∞∞

"Stop your fighting, and know that I am God, exalted among the nations,
exalted on the earth." PSALM 46:10

Remember that God is God and we are not.
May you find rest as you rely on Him.

Words of Life That
Celebrate Love

Her shoulders sagged under the weight only she knew she was carrying. Worries about grades, career, and (heaviest of all) relationships wreaked havoc on her mind and heart, leaving her longing for peace. The demands she put on herself to perform well and please others in order to both succeed in the workplace and earn acceptance wearied her soul. *What would happen if I fail?* she secretly worried. *Would I lose their respect and love?*

This concern plagues every person who longs to be loved unconditionally. Yet we live in a world full of fickle fans whose self-serving love often disappears when they don't like what they see. It's no wonder our insecurities abound.

But God is not like us human beings. He will never withdraw His *agape* love for us, no matter what mistakes we make. His affection is a sure foundation for every member of His forever family, and the security we find in His love helps us through our own ups and downs in life.

As God's children, we have the distinct privilege of reminding one another just how precious we are in our Father's eyes, not because of what we've done, but because of who He is. May the Father's love flow to and through us, His children!

"I give you a new command:
Love one another.
Just as I have loved you,
you are also to love
one another. By this
everyone will know that
you are My disciples,
if you love one another."

John 13:34-35

Life-Giving Words That *Celebrate Love*

Dear friends, let us love one another, because love is from God, and everyone who loves has been born of God and knows God. I JOHN 4:7

I feel God's love in the way you care for me.

∞∞∞∞∞∞∞∞

Set me as a seal on your heart, as a seal on your arm. For love is as strong as death; jealousy is as unrelenting as Sheol. Love's flames are fiery flames— an almighty flame! SONG OF SOLOMON 8:6

I am fully committed to you. No matter what happens, I'm not going anywhere. I will be by your side.

∞∞∞∞∞∞∞∞

You, Lord, are a compassionate and gracious God, slow to anger and abounding in faithful love and truth. PSALM 86:15

Don't be afraid to turn to God anytime, about anything. The cross not only revealed His compassion and grace, but it cleared the path for us to experience the full weight and warmth of His abounding love.

∞∞∞∞∞∞∞∞

If I speak human or angelic tongues but do not have love, I am a noisy gong or a clanging cymbal. If I have the gift of prophecy and understand all mysteries and all knowledge, and if I have all faith so that I can move mountains but do not have love, I am nothing. And if I give away all my possessions, and if I give over my body in order to boast but do not have love, I gain nothing. I CORINTHIANS 13:1-3

Working in our own strength is a waste of time. But the agape love of God flowing into us and through us adds good to everything.

190

The LORD your God is living among you. He is a mighty savior.
He will take delight in you with gladness. With His love, He will calm all
your fears. He will rejoice over you with joyful songs." ZEPHANIAH 3:17 NLT

Your Savior sings over you with joy! With gratitude,
relax in the shelter of His unending love.

✕✕✕✕✕✕✕✕✕✕✕✕

Let love be without hypocrisy. Detest evil; cling to what is good.
Love one another deeply as brothers and sisters.
Outdo one another in showing honor. ROMANS 12:9-10

You have an amazing ability to make every person
you talk to feel important and valued.
What a blessing and joy you are to so many of us!

✕✕✕✕✕✕✕✕✕✕✕✕

Love never ends. I CORINTHIANS 13:8

The story of God's love for us never has a final chapter.
His love for us will go on forever!

✕✕✕✕✕✕✕✕✕✕✕✕

Do not owe anyone anything, except to love one another,
for the one who loves another has fulfilled the law. ROMANS 13:8

No need to return the favor!. I'm did it because I love you!

✕✕✕✕✕✕✕✕✕✕✕✕

I had just passed them when I found the one I love. I held on
to him and would not let him go. SONG OF SOLOMON 3:4

God loves you more than you can even imagine.
And He will never let you go.

191

LIVE YOUR FAITH

Dear Friend,

This book was prayerfully crafted with you, the reader, in mind—every word, every sentence, every page—was thoughtfully written, designed, and packaged to encourage you...right where you are this very moment. At DaySpring, our vision is to see every person experience the life-changing message of God's love. So, as we worked through rough drafts, design changes, edits and details, we prayed for you to deeply experience His unfailing love, indescribable peace, and pure joy. It is our sincere hope that through these Truth-filled pages your heart will be blessed, knowing that God cares about you—your desires and disappointments, your challenges and dreams.

He knows. He cares. He loves you unconditionally.

BLESSINGS!
THE DAYSPRING BOOK TEAM